The Angry Liberal's Handbook of Economics

By

Benedict Arbutiski

authorHOUSE™

1663 LIBERTY DRIVE, SUITE 200
BLOOMINGTON, INDIANA 47403
(800) 839-8640
WWW.AUTHORHOUSE.COM

First published by AuthorHouse 07/22/04

ISBN: 1-4184-1704-1 (e)
ISBN: 1-4184-1703-3 (sc)

Printed in the United States of America
Bloomington, Indiana

This book is printed on acid-free paper.

Table of Contents

Forward

I was born a Democrat in 1942, son of a coal miner in western Pennsylvania. My father loved Harry Truman, and hated Dwight Eisenhower, simply because the former was a Democrat, and the latter was a Republican. My mother was also a devoted Democrat, and was involved in local politics, doing whatever volunteer work she could to support the party.

My mother was an avid reader. She particularly liked Readers Digest because it gave her an overview of all the important things going on in the world around us. One day when my older brother and I were still in grade school, she read an article about college financial aid for working-class kids. She learned there were such things as scholarships and low-interest loans for poor kids who made good grades in school. She read, in another article, that even more scholarships were available if you were an athlete, in particular a football player. She made the decisions at that time that her boys were (1) going to get good grades, namely A's in school, and (2) going to play football, starting in middle school. My brother and I duly quit the band upon leaving elementary school, and did her bidding. She sweetened the deal by giving us a dollar for every A we made, quite a lot of money in those days.

I subsequently graduated high school, and went to Cornell University on a full engineering scholarship. I did play football, but only one year, as I needed to devote all of my time to maintain an 80% grade average to keep the scholarship. Besides, I was not very big, and was getting pulverized daily on the practice field.

After getting my five-year chemical engineering degree in 1965, I joined the Mobil Oil Corporation as a research engineer. Several years later, I got really bored, and enrolled at the Wharton Business School. Armed with an MBA in 1970, and resolved never to be bored again, I rejoined Mobil, and relocated to a job in an oil refinery in the Netherlands. I ended up working for Mobil for over thirty years, living twice in Germany, and traveling all over the world as a consultant for the overseas affiliates. My main areas of concentration were oil refineries and large projects. I got involved not only in the technical side of things, but also in business and management issues. Near the end of my career, one of my associates from Australia referred to me as "Mr. Fixit". I was truly flattered.

I am now retired and writing a book—the one you are about to read, and hopefully finish.

Now, why did I write this book? I have strong liberal leanings. Not only was I born a Democrat, but I have an autistic son, which showed me how important it can be to have the help of others. Besides my two natural-born children, I have adopted, along with my second wife, a teenage boy from Honduras. Only a true liberal would do something like that.

I am not only a liberal. I am also upset, angry, as the title of this book indicates. Why? Over the years, I have lost much of my faith in our beloved Democrat party. This feeling turned into disgust when I listened to Al Gore's speech at the 2000 Democratic presidential convention. It was a compilation of populist nonsense, culminating with his pointing at me and saying, "I want to help YOU." Hell, I didn't want him to help me. I wanted him to run the strongest country in the world, in an efficient and forthright manner. I wrote him a letter immediately, and started it by saying, "Dear Al, if you don't listen to me, you will lose the election." He didn't listen to me, and didn't even thank me for the advice in the letter!

Well, as history has shown, Al lost the election, in part because I helped George Bush win by giving him my vote. That's not the first time that I voted for a Republican. I also voted for Bob Dole, because I felt Bill Clinton was a sleazy person, and would get himself into trouble. And that he did! Party loyalty is very important to me, but the health of my country comes first.'

My reasons for writing this book are simple. Al Gore, Tom Daschle, and most of the top democrats are hopeless on economic policy. The populist stuff—the anti-corporate, anti-wealth posturing doesn't work anymore. Our citizens are becoming more educated and sophisticated, and most families are investing in the stock market, either directly or indirectly via private pension plans. Democrats want to own stocks, and they want their kids to be rich. Nevertheless, you still have democratic leaders like John Edwards and John Kerry spouting anti-trade, anti-wealth speeches as if they were addressing voters of the 1950's or 1960's.

I am convinced that many of our Democrat leaders, and most of my liberal friends, really do not understand how our economic system works. As a consequence the Democrats have not developed a positive, rational, coherent economic policy. Rather, the leaders address economic issues by uttering a bunch of negative, griping sound bites. Four years later, in election year 2004, things haven't changed much, in my opinion.

Therefore, I am writing this book to educate my liberal friends and associates on how our economic system works, and to give them some concrete ideas and policies on really important issues such as economic growth, social security, immigration, tax reform, education, and energy policy. Perhaps most importantly, I want to inspire our junior liberals— those young men and women who care deeply about our country and the welfare of other people. If we don't win in 2004, maybe they can help us win in later years.

You might ask about my qualifications for writing such a book. I'm not an economist, after all. That's true, but it is probably an advantage. Instead of getting a PhD in economics, and working in an isolated think-tank environment, I have been working out there in the real world for more than thirty years. I have both technical and business degrees, and I have studied business and political practices in more than 20 countries. The oil business is, after all, a geo-political business. You learn a lot if you keep your eyes and mind open, more than a PhD degree would offer. Also, you need that learning to successfully operate in those countries. So yes, I think I am qualified to write such a book. You can be the ultimate judge.

My intent was not to write a textbook, but rather a book with a simple, conversational tone, with a little fun thrown in to keep you awake. I have tried to use everyday language so that you can pick up the concepts quickly. I have tried to keep the chapters short and concise so that you don't get too bored or bogged down in jargon. I hope I have succeeded, and I hope you enjoy it!

Chapter 1. Introduction. The Master Equation

Everyone thinks that economic theory is very complicated, and that the average person cannot possibly understand it. That is indeed the experience for many people who open any standard economic textbook and start to read it. You become quickly bored and your mind becomes like molasses and resists every paragraph. Actually, the basic stuff--the important stuff-- is not that complicated, and it's not boring. If you put a bit of effort into it, you can figure out a lot of important things. You can become a better citizen. You can determine whether your elected officials are trying to feed you sense or nonsense.

Let's start with a simple statement of fact. The total output of a country--the total production of goods and services--is determined by the number of workers and how productive they are. We can express this thought in a simple equation:

Output = Number of Workers x Average Worker Productivity

What use is such an equation? Well, it gives you a lot of useful insights if you start thinking about it. Let's look at some situations.

First of all, let's assume that the government suddenly reduces the retirement age of all workers. If you look at the above equation, the number of workers immediately decreases. Therefore, the national output declines. There are fewer goods and services produced in the country. The remaining active workers are hit by a double whammy. There are

1

fewer goods and services to share, and they have more retirees to support. Everybody's standard of living goes down. What a mess! You can see why there is no movement underway to reduce official retirement age in the US. In fact it was raised some years ago from 65 to 70. So there. You learned something already.

Let's look at a related case, this time a really serious situation. In most developed countries (i.e., US, Europe, and Japan), birth rates are much lower than in the past. At the same time, people are living longer. If you go down the road twenty years or so, you could have a very difficult situation developing. The number of active workers could actually decrease, while the number of retired folks increases. Looking at the above equation, national output will decrease--if average worker productivity doesn't keep up with the loss of workers. That means the economic pie will get smaller--total production of goods and services will decline. Each active worker will be getting less because he will be supporting more retired folks. In effect, his taxes will have to go up, to provide support to the retirees. He will have less for himself and his family. At some point, social unrest could result. Also, the ability of the country to defend itself will also decline, because there will be less productive capacity in the country, and fewer potential young soldiers.

What are the solutions for this situation? Well, we could decrease social security benefits for retirees, and create a larger class of poor, elderly people. But that replaces one problem by another, and certainly does nothing to strengthen the nation. There are other ways to solve these problems. This subject will be covered separately in Chapter 7, because it is so important to our country's future, and cannot be addressed in a few short paragraphs. However, I promise you that it will be handled simply enough so that you can understand it.

Let's look now at a shorter-term problem. At the time I am writing this book, we are emerging from a so-called economic recession, and the national unemployment rate is still high, pushing 6 %. At many times in the past, it was actually much higher, and right now in several European nations, it is close to 10%. What is the impact of higher unemployment? Well, every worker who is unemployed has a productivity of zero, because he's not working, right? Employers will push the remaining active workers to work harder. Nevertheless, increases in unemployment will finally result in a reduction in average worker productivity, because so many of them are doing nothing. When it reaches this point, the master equation predicts that the national output will go down. Now, that's what economists call a recession. Actually, being very precise, they define a recession as a period of three consecutive quarters of a year of negative growth of a thing call GNP. Go figure. I consider any period of increased unemployment as a recession, because it hurts people, they lose their jobs. And to me this is a nation of people, not GNP's. But we are here to help solve problems, not pick on economists. So how do we decrease unemployment?. Again, that is a very important issue, and it deserves a full chapter of clear analysis and discussion. So we will address that matter in Chapter 8.

All right, this chapter is getting long, and I promised you short concise chapters, didn't I. So we will discuss only one more problem to illustrate the use of the master equation. Let's pick a really bad case. Suppose we had a war, on our own soil, such that many workers became soldiers and were killed. Also, let's assume that much of our country was destroyed,--in particular, many industrial factories, transportation equipment, and much of our infrastructure.

Whoops, what is infrastructure? It's a good word to know for the rest of your life, so time out for a brief explanation. It is all the stuff that the government and industry has built to promote commerce and travel--highways, bridges, power plants, government buildings, and so on. Get the picture? Okay, let's go on.

Now, under these conditions, several bad things have happened. Some workers have become soldiers, and got killed. Some other workers did not become soldiers, but they were killed anyhow, too, during the fighting. (Some military types refer to these poor souls as "collateral damage". Just a little extraneous info in case you've seen the term used, but didn't know what it means.) Okay, then, overall, we have lost a lot of workers. Referring to our master equation, national output would decrease because we have permanently lost many workers. If we lost 20% of our workers, output would decrease also by roughly 20%.

But that's only part of the problem here. Let's not forget all of the destroyed factories, equipment, and infrastructure. These things are extremely important, because they LEVERAGE the work input of a person. Kind of like a shovel leverages a person's ability to dig a hole, versus doing it with his hands. Suppose I told you to build a pair of shoes, a good pair, and deliver it to my aunt in Texas without the benefit of factories and infrastructure. It would take you a lot of time to make the shoes from

3

scratch, to walk to Texas to make the delivery, and then walk back home. Well, when you have factories, equipment and infrastructure, a whole lot of people do the same task with much less overall time and effort than you could do it alone. In effect, then, factories, equipment and infrastructure increase the productivity of workers tremendously.

Anyhow, we have lost a lot of factories, equipment and infrastructure. Let's assume we lost half of these facilities, for illustrative purposes, okay? And let's assume further that the remaining active workers have lost half their productivity as a result. (Economic theory makes a lot of assumptions, so I'm only doing what I'm supposed to do.) Referring to the master equation, with only 80 % of our active workers remaining, and their productivity cut to 50%, national output would drop to 40% of the pre-war level. That's a dramatic decline, and everyone would suffer, getting only 40% of the goods and services that they did before the war started.

Obviously, war is a horrible thing. The example we just went through is not as bad as it was in several European countries after World War II. And today many countries are in bad shape due to war. Afghanistan, Liberia, Sierra Leone, Angola, Palestine, Chechnya (the latter two are not countries, but want to be). And the list goes on. Bosnia, Croatia, Colombia, Iraq, etc.

If I kept my promise, this would be the end of Chapter 1. However, I must break my promise because there is something more I want to address before we go on. It adds several more chapters to this book, which will make it look more impressive. So what is it? It's more about productivity. You learned that many things add to the productivity of an average worker-- factories, equipment (e.g., bulldozers, trucks, computers, and the like), and infrastructure (I already explained that). How about education? Very important. We'll have a chapter that discusses that in more detail. How about organizations? Now you would ask, "What organizations?" Almost all goods and services produced in this country come from COMPANIES and CORPORATIONS. These are organizations, licensed by other organizations called GOVERNMENT, and regulated by those same organizations-- government. Actually, there are several types of government, all of which affect the behavior of corporations. They are basically city, county, state and federal governments. For our purposes, we will mainly refer to them as just plain "government", unless something comes up that requires us to distinguish among them. Okay?

Anyhow our government likes to license a lot of corporations, such that many of them produce the same or similar things. Like gasoline. Like Pepsi and Coke. Why is this good? We'll tell you later, but it has something to do with competition. Why do we have corporations at all? Why doesn't the government produce everything? That's scary. Remember the Soviet Union? We'll discuss that later, too. Wait a minute, let's not forget labor unions. They are organizations also that have had a lot of impact on our economy. We'll look at them, too. Lots of good stuff here, and food for several chapters. Let's end this one right now, as you're probably dying to go to the bathroom. I am.

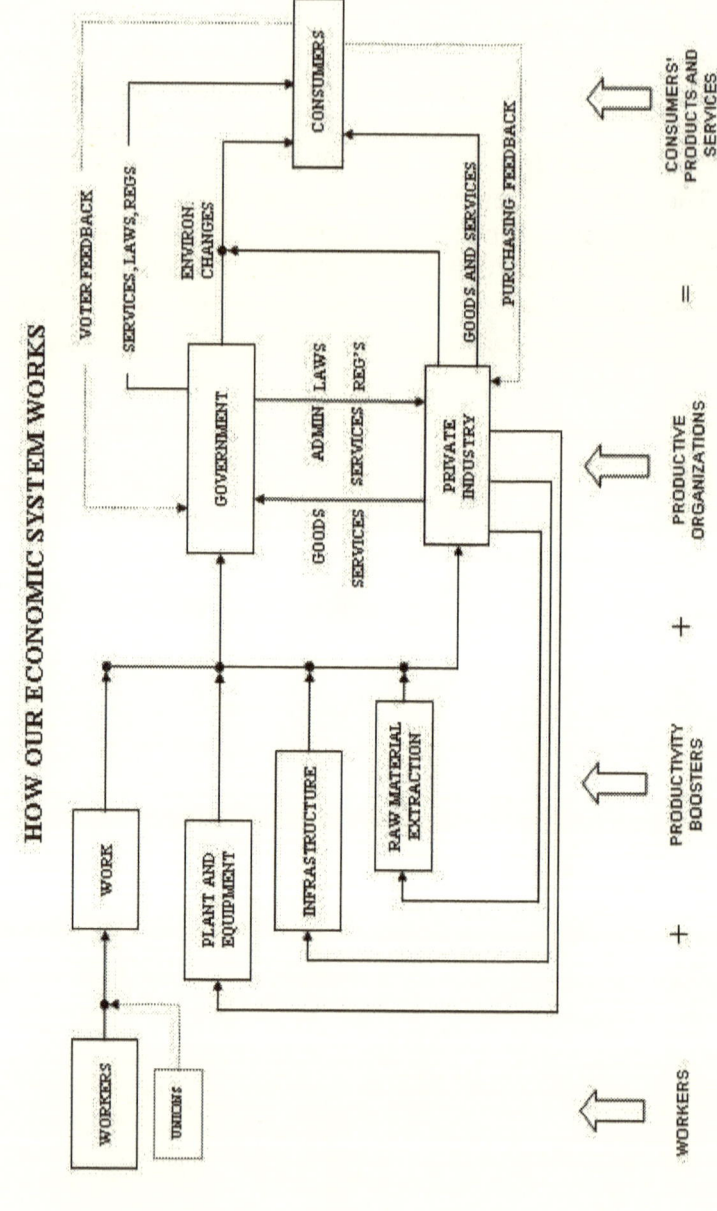

HOW OUR ECONOMIC SYSTEM WORKS

Chapter 2. Our Economic System

In the previous chapter, you got a rough idea how our economy works. In this chapter, we will look at our economy in more detail to give you a better idea. You'll notice that I have included a complicated-looking diagram on the opposite page to help you out. It's really not so bad, once you get into it. So, let's do an overview first.

On the far left side of the diagram, you have workers. They put into the economic system something called work. That's all, just work. Way on the right side, you have consumers, who get a lot of things from the economic system. Things like cars, shoes, houses, and computers. Things like electricity, clean water, and phone service. They also get direct services from talented people, such as plumbers, electricians, teachers, entertainers, and parents.

What?? Parents?? Of course, parents. Parenting is hard work-- hard, unpaid work. Parents are growing the workers of the future. Kids are consumers of parents' hard labor. It's important, and it isn't easy. There are good and bad parents, just as there are good and bad carpenters. Okay, enough about parents, for now.

Anyhow, all of these products and services that are available to us come from (1) work and (2) our economic system. You have workers on one end, and consumers on the other, with the economic system in the middle. By the way, if you haven't guessed already, workers and consumers are the same people. They are us! Part of the day we work, and part of the day we consume. If you consume, but don't work, you must be a kid or a retiree. If you are neither, you should get your butt to work and do your part!

Now let's look in the middle, where all the boxes are located. That's where things happen, that's the economic system. Work is combined with three other things--(1) plant and equipment, (2) infrastructure, and (3) "raw material extraction". These are called "productivity boosters". Raw material extraction, by the way, includes farms, mines, fishing boats, and other facilities that recover raw materials from the earth and seas. The other two boosters we've already discussed in Chapter 1. Anyhow, work and these three boosters are used by "productive organizations"-- private industry and government-- to make or provide what the consumers want or need. Besides the obvious things, such as the goods and services mentioned earlier, the productive organizations produce other things we may or may not want. The government box gives us laws and regulations, and protective services such as police, fire fighters, and, of course, the military. Working together, government and private industry also give us something called environmental changes. These could be good or bad. They are the changes in the quality of our air, water, and landscape that result from changes in government regulations imposed on private industry, and from changes in the productivity boosters operated by private industry.

One thing that I want you to notice about the diagram is that the only goods and services that count are those that are finally consumed by the consumer. Most economists prefer another way of thinking that focuses on GNP (Gross National Product). GNP includes not only the goods and services consumed by consumers, but also those consumed by private industry and government as well. Is GNP a better way of looking at the economy? Think about it. If the Postal Service orders 100 trucks, when it could have gotten by with 50, that is just fine. It all goes into GNP. If the Pentagon orders 100 fighter planes when 50 would have been enough, that's just fine, too. It all goes into GNP. If Exxon/Mobil orders five executive jets, when it could have gotten by with one or none, that's okay. It all goes into GNP. As you can plainly see, it's not okay, because all the resources that were used to make these unnecessary products could have been used instead to make products for the consumer. In this country, it's the consumer, the citizen, who is most important. Government and private industry are there to serve the citizen in the most efficient manner. Don't forget that.

So, that's a quick overview of the economic system. Its purpose is to maximize gross consumer product, to make the most and best products and services for the citizens. Now let's go over it again, but in somewhat more detail. Stop that moaning! Get a cup of coffee, or go to the bathroom. But come back!

First of all, let's look again at that thing called "work". The QUALITY of that work is an extremely important issue. It affects the productivity of the workers. You want an electrician who is doing a job for you to be BOTH well-trained and motivated so that he does the job as quickly and efficiently as possible. After all, these guys are expensive, and they're paid by the hour! The faster he completes a job, the less he costs per job, and the more jobs he can do in a day, which makes his employer happy, too. Similarly, you want a teacher to be well-trained and motivated, so that each kid learns as much as possible every day. The overall message here is that if you want an economy that is the best in the world, you need a work force that is well-trained and motivated to work hard and efficiently. Do not ever forget that.

Next, let's look again at the three productivity boosters --plant and equipment, infrastructure, and raw materials extraction. You will note that they are all created by private industry. Many of these facilities are very expensive, and take a long time to build. For example, an oil refinery that produces gasoline, diesel fuel, lubricants, etc. may cost as much as a billion dollars, and take up to five years to design and build. Likewise a modern steel plant. Why are they so big and expensive? Because, generally speaking, the bigger they are, the cheaper the product--be it a gallon of gasoline, a kilowatt of electricity, or a ton of steel. That's called "economies of scale" by the economists.

As indicated in Chapter 1, these productive boosters are extremely important, because they magnify the productivity of workers and thus the strength of the economy. Money investments are required every year in these boosters--not only to create new facilities to accommodate a growing economy, but also to modernize what has already been built. In a vibrant economy like the US, these boosters become more efficient year after year, and raise the productivity of workers, year after year.

Now let's move on to the two "productive organizations"--private industry and government. You will note that private industry is at the middle of everything. It consists of thousands of corporations and private companies that can employ anywhere from one person to hundreds of thousands of people. Private industry produces the vast majority of goods and services consumed in the country. Not only does it produce virtually everything that you buy, but also what the government uses. That includes military equipment such as guns, submarines, fighter planes, and missiles. It is true that the government is in charge of planning, operating, and maintaining some things, like bridges, defense facilities, buildings, and the Houston Space Center, but most of the work in these facilities is actually contracted out to private companies. That's because private companies usually do things more efficiently because they are exposed to competition. (There's that word again, competition; it's very important, and we'll be mentioning it often.)

You might ask at this point why I have named government as one of the two "productive organizations". You have undoubtedly heard or read that government is inefficient, bloated, unresponsive to citizens' needs, and blah, blah, blah. That is true sometimes for government but it is true sometimes for industry as well. In either case, there are mechanisms in our economic system for correcting such defects. In the case of industry, there is competition, as I have mentioned. In addition, if you refer again to our diagram in this chapter, there is "purchasing feedback" from consumers. So, if you are a company, you must be cost-efficient, because of competition from other companies. Furthermore, you must produce what consumers want at a reasonable price and good quality, or they will take their business elsewhere. Not much room for laxity or laziness there. We'll discuss this issue in more detail later in the book.

Turning back to government, we have two main control mechanisms to affect its performance, which I refer to as "voter feedback". The media (television, newspapers, radio, etc.) constantly watch the performance of our politicians, and keep us informed. If we find out that someone is not doing a good job, we can vote him out of office the next time around. This is an important power for us citizens, because good government is critical for a healthy economy. This is such an important issue that I have devoted a few chapters to various government policies and responsibilities. More on that later.

Someone might have noticed that I have not mentioned labor unions yet. Well, I will devote some time to them right now. Their main purpose is to represent workers on such issues as wages and working conditions. Labor unions have played a critical role in the past, particularly during the first half of the 20th century. Among their many achievements are the establishment of the eight-hour working day, abolishment of child labor, vast improvements in safety practices, payroll benefits such as subsidized medical insurance, and establishment of minimum wage laws. Union influence was also important in the creation of the Labor Department of the US government, which enforces federal labor laws and regulations. Union pressure was vital in the establishment of the Occupational Health and Safety Administration (OSHA), which is part of the Labor Department. OSHA's responsibilities are kind of obvious from its name. It makes sure that work environments across the country are consistent with our laws. Part of OSHA's duties are to inspect suspect worksites to insure that companies are complying with those laws.

Perhaps you have an uneasy feeling about now. Why are unions necessary? Why were they created in the first place? Later in the book we will talk more about companies and corporations and competition. You will learn that companies will do almost anything to improve profits. They will squeeze workers as much as possible to get the most from them. In the early 20th century, things got so bad, that workers started to form unions and stage strikes. Occasionally, violent strikes occurred, with workers pitted against goons hired by the companies. Eventually, the federal government decided to take action, and passed various labor relations laws to protect unions and the rights of workers.

Over time, this effort has been quite successful. So successful, in fact, that the union movement has almost put itself out of business. In 1950, about 35% of workers were union members. Today, less than 15% are members. With regard to the future, it is difficult to judge what will happen. Unions do not have a great reputation right now. Some of them, such as longshoremen (dock workers) and Teamsters (truckers) have been associated in the past with organized crime. In some industries, particularly airlines, unions have been blamed for pushing costs so high that companies have gone into bankruptcy. In some cases, companies have shut down plants in highly unionized areas and built new ones in non-union locations to keep costs down. In Washington, DC, the head of the public teachers union has been accused, with others, of misusing millions of dollars in union funds. The Democrat party has been accused by others (i.e., Republicans) of pandering to the unions, which make large money contributions to the Democrat's election campaigns. The Republicans claim that the money comes from union members' dues, and the members have no control or vote regarding the use of that money. In conclusion, it is a rocky time for the union movement, and who knows how it will all end up. The tug and push of democracy will be the final determinant. But you can be sure of one thing. Unions will be there in some form to protect the rights of workers.

So, it would appear that we're done with this chapter. Well, not quite. I have to tell you a little story first that illustrates some of the concepts we've discussed so far. In late 2002, I was reading an article about Germany in the Economist magazine, my favorite periodical. You will recall that Germany used to be two countries. West Germany was pretty much an open economy like the US. East Germany was part of the Soviet bloc, and had a communist economy. It had a socialist-type government, in which all industry was owned and operated by the government, and the government was pretty much a dictatorship. Get the picture? Well, in the early 1990's, the two countries merged, the West took over, and the communist system was junked. Well, it was really tough for the East part of the country (the Ossies) to accommodate themselves to the new system. Old inefficient plants were shut down, thousands of people lost their jobs. However, the Wessies helped out by investing billions of dollars (Deutsche Marks, actually) in new plants and infrastructure there, and retraining the Ossies. After ten years or so, most Ossies are doing just fine, and the productivity of the economy has improved dramatically. For example, the Ossies now produce the same amount of agricultural output with one tenth the size of the original farm work force. Similarly, they make the same amount of steel with one-fifth the number of workers. All the other people have been freed up to do other jobs elsewhere in the economy. Isn't that cool?

Get the picture? I hope so. As they used to say when I was young, if you are a college student, and you are not a communist, you have no heart. If you are 35 years old, and are still a communist, you have no brain.

Chapter 3. Incomes, Spending, and Saving

Welcome back. I know you're looking at the title of this chapter and wondering, what's this all about? Well, so far we have constructed an efficient economy, full of highly trained, motivated workers, which is spewing out large amounts of valuable goods and services. Now the question is, how do we split it up? How do you get your fair share?

First of all, we need an efficient way for workers who make shoes, for example, to get food. You will not find one such worker walking into a grocery store and trying to buy food in exchange for a pair of shoes that he has made. Instead we have something called "money", created and provided by the government. We'll talk later about how the government does that, but right now let's assume it's already done. Let's assume further that the government does a good job of controlling the amount of money in the economy so that it is valuable. Valuable enough, let's say, so that, with $400, I can go buy an ounce of gold, which is the case at the present time. Got that? Okay.

Now, this guy wants to buy some food. As you recall, he works in a shoe factory. Every two weeks, he gets a paycheck for all the shoes he helped make. He goes to a bank, and cashes the check. His bank, in turn, contacts the bank of the shoe factory, which takes money from the shoe factory's account, and transfers it to the worker's bank, which then puts it into the worker's account. The worker now has money, and he can go buy food--or anything else he wants--until his bank account is empty. He then has to stop buying things until his next pay check. Actually, he does have another option. He can borrow some money. But if he does that, he will have to pay it back later. Also, when you borrow money, you have to pay interest. Borrowing money can get you into a lot of trouble, but sometimes it makes sense. More on that later.

Okay, now we have money in the economy, and it circulates round and round, going from one bank account to another. Money is actually the blood stream of the economy! No kidding, it is! If you somehow would remove all the money, the economy would stop dead.

Okay, let's get back to the issue of splitting up the booty--all those goods and services produced by the economy. Here's how it's done. Everyone gets a certain amount of money--it's called income-- and spends some of it. Where do they get the money? Most people get it by working. They get wages and salaries. Wages and salaries are called "active income". Why? Because people work to get it. Well, if there is active income, there must be inactive income, right? Yes. But it's called "passive income". People who get passive income don't do anything for it, but get paid anyhow. You're probably thinking, what a deal! How do I get in on it? Well, there is a catch, because if you have it, you, or someone who loves you, earned a right to it at an earlier time. That right is called an "entitlement". Like you are entitled to get that income. Got that? Okay.

However, you might say, I don't know anyone who gets paid an "entitlement", I've never seen that word before, and neither have my friends. Actually entitlement is a fancy word that is used for the following types of income, which we will discuss briefly below: pensions, social security, Medicare, interest, dividends, welfare benefits, and Medicaid.

Let's look first at pensions, social security, and Medicare, since they are similar. When a person works, certain amounts of money are removed from his paycheck right away, so he can't get his hands on it. The government takes out income tax, social security tax, and Medicare tax. Income tax is his contribution to the cost of running the government. Bye, bye forever. Social security and Medicare taxes are taken out now, but with a promise from the government to pay you back later--when you are retired. So, when you are retired, you get a monthly social security check, and you get some free health care, called Medicare. Sounds fair, right?

Let's get back to pensions. They are the same as social security, but the money is deducted from your paycheck by your employer when you are working, and when you retire, the employer gives you monthly retirement checks.

So, if your employer has a pension plan (some don't), you will get two monthly checks when you are retired--one from social security, and one from your former employer. Plus you get some free medical care called Medicare. Medicare doesn't cover everything, like all prescription drugs (at least, not yet), but does cover some basic health care.

It's important to notice something at this point. When you are employed and paying social security and Medicare taxes, you don't get any of those benefits. You are actually paying benefits for those people currently retired. Likewise, when you finally get old and decrepit, and retire, the younger generation of workers will be paying for your benefits. We'll get into this issue in more detail in Chapter 7. It's very important.

Now, let's look at interest and dividends. They come from direct saving of money. Let's assume that you put aside money every month into some kind of savings account. Initially, it could be a simple savings account in a bank, which pays a certain amount of interest. It will build up over time, as you add money every month, and the bank pays interest to you every month. When you accumulate enough money in that account, you can put a chunk of it into something that pays higher interest, such as a CD (certificate of deposit) or a bond. Or you can become part owner of a corporation, by buying stocks in that company. If the company pays dividends, you can reinvest the dividends to buy more stock, or bonds, or whatever you want.

All of these things--savings accounts, CD's, bonds, and stocks are called investments. You invest your money into them, and later on you have an entitlement to collect all the interest and dividends. Also, you can sell the stock, bond, or CD, or cash in the savings account and use that money to buy things or services. You save or invest money, and get to spend it later. The borrowers make it sweeter by paying interest and dividends. Also, most stocks go up in value with time, because most companies grow with time, and as a part-owner, your share increases in value. Cool, huh? But as I mentioned earlier, you have to save money to take advantage of these things. Or, as I indicated earlier, if someone loves you and they have money, they can buy these things for you. Not everyone is so lucky.

The last types of entitlement we will discuss are welfare benefits, Medicaid, and Supplemental Social Security. These are cash payments, food stamps, and medical care that are provided by government to poor people and people with severe handicaps. People are poor for a number of reasons. The parents might be unemployed for a while, a temporary situation. One or both parents might be mentally or physically handicapped, which can be a permanent situation. The family might have only one parent and one or more kids, which is a long-term situation. Finally, one or both parents might be unemployable. They are either unable or unwilling to get out of bed in the morning, show up for work on time, and perform some type of productive work. Whatever the case, the families or individuals can apply for welfare, Medicaid, or Supplementary Social Security from the government. It is worth mentioning at this point that state and federal governments have made some recent major changes to their policies in this area, which make it harder to get benefits. More about that in Chapter 11.

So, let's summarize all this stuff. The economy is churning out goods and services. People are getting money to buy their share of the economic pie. They get money from working or from their entitlement stockpile, or both. They spend most of it on those goods and services that suit them, and save the rest, if there is anything left over. It's that simple.

Guess what? We're finished with this chapter. There is a lot of really important info here. I hope you were able to follow it all. If not, go back and read it again. It's that important. And it's not that difficult to understand.

Chapter 4. Corporations, Companies, and Competition.

So you want to learn more about corporations. No? You think you know enough already? What do you know? Like, corporations are big companies. They make lots of money for the rich fat cats, who gobble up most of the dividends and interest that companies pay. Like they cheat investors. Sure, look at Enron, World Com, Global Crossing, Tyco and Adelphia. Hey, don't forget the big bosses in those corporations--they make bags of money and fly around in fancy jets and smoke big fat expensive cigars. And they mistreat workers. Yeah, right! Look at all the layoffs going on right now all over the country.

Yes, yes, yes, there is truth in all this, but that is not the whole picture about corporations. I will try to give it to you. I will try to convince you that corporations are in fact good for you and good for America. As money is the bloodstream of the economy, companies and corporations are the vital organs of the economy. However, I will also tell you that they have to be watched. They can turn bad, and become cancerous, in a way. Sometimes, if they get bad enough, they are excised from the body of the economy. We'll discuss all that later.

But, first of all, what is a company, or a corporation? They are organizations licensed by the government to produce and sell goods and services. I will not distinguish between companies and corporations, because they are not much different. They can be owned either privately or publicly, and can be any size. For tax reasons, some doctors set themselves up as corporations. Now that is a small business! You have the doctor, maybe two, and a receptionist as employees. That's it. At the other extreme, you have mega-companies like the oil giant, Exxon-Mobil or Wal-Mart, which employ tens of thousands of people around the world, and earn over a billion dollars a year. The vast majority of companies and corporations are somewhere in the middle.

What do I mean by "publicly owned"? Basically, it means that you or I can buy ownership in such a company, simply by buying some stock. Privately-owned companies, by contrast, are just that, they are owned completely by individuals, and you can't buy into them.

It is worth pointing out that most privately-owned companies are quite small. Many new jobs in our economy are created by this group of companies. Most of them provide goods and services to larger corporations. Many of them fail. However, some of them grow up to become large corporations themselves, if they are successful. Examples of relatively new and successful corporations are Microsoft, Cisco, Yahoo, JetBlue, and Amazon.com. Twenty years ago, none of these companies existed!

It is also worth noting that when small companies become larger corporations, they are usually run by professional managers. Sometimes the original founders stay on for awhile (like Bill Gates at Microsoft and Jeff Bezos at Amazon.com), but eventually they are replaced by professional managers (as Steve Case recently was at AOL Time/Warner--now simply Time/Warner).

Okay, what do corporations actually do? They sell products or services. They also make money for the owners, called profits. The profits are used in three ways. First of all, the profits can be used to expand the company. Or they can be used to modernize what they already have. Finally, they can be paid out to stockholders as dividends. Many companies do all three.

What if a company loses money? This is bad. If they keep doing it, they have to go out of business. In effect, the company dies. Usually, they are given a second chance, called Title 11 bankruptcy. What happens in Title 11 bankruptcy is that virtually all debts are "reconstructed", with lower interest rates and stretched-out payments. This, of course makes the lenders very upset. That's why companies who lend money, like banks, are very careful when giving out loans. They want to be sure that the person or company borrowing the money can pay it back--on time and in the right amount.

So why would a company take such a chance and borrow money at all? Actually, almost all companies borrow money from time to time. Why? Usually because they think they see a good opportunity. For example, sometimes they can't make anymore of a certain product in a factory, yet they know they can sell more. In that case, if they don't have enough money on hand, they will borrow some money and then invest their own money and the borrowed money into a new factory. They are assuming that the extra money they make in the new factory every year will be more than the money they need to pay back the loan. Usually, this is the way it works. Why? Because the people who run the company know the business well, and they study the situation carefully before they finally decide to make the investment.

In the same way, investments can be made to improve existing equipment. For example, instead of putting in a new factory, the company can sometimes expand an existing factory. Usually, this is much cheaper and less risky. Also, companies make investments to reduce costs, like electricity consumption, and fuel consumption. Sometimes, they make investments to reduce the cost of manpower. This means they will need fewer employees, fewer people. That means some people will have to leave the company. Some people will leave voluntarily, like those people who go into retirement, or those people who quit to find better jobs. Other people will leave because they are laid off or fired.

This is the sad part. Every day, corporations somewhere in the country are laying off people. Why? Because they are trying to reduce their costs. Well, why are they doing that? Because they have to be competitive. What does that mean? Why is it important?

In order to understand this better, we have to look at the financial situation of a company. Now, don't be scared off. It's really quite simple and easy to understand.

Every year, a company makes "revenues". This is money from selling their goods and services. In order to produce and deliver those goods and services, they have costs. If the revenues in a year are more than the costs, the corporation makes a profit for the year, which is simply the revenues minus the costs. Got that? Good. Quite simple actually.

Before we go on, we should look at all the types of costs that corporations have--the types of bills they have to pay. Some of them you already know. Let's make a list.

-Electricity
-Fuel (e.g., oil products, coal ,and natural gas)
-Chemicals and other supplies
-Manpower, which includes:
    -Wages and Salaries
    -Employee Benefits (social security, pensions, medical, etc.)
-Maintenance of equipment and buildings
-Taxes (Local, state, and federal. Just like a person!)
-Insurance
-Cost of loans, which includes:
    -Principle (Pay back part of what you borrowed, e.g., 5%/year)
    -Interest (Pay some % of what you still owe, e.g., 8%/year)

There may be more items, depending on the company, but this gives you an idea. Lots of bills to pay! And the money from revenues must be earned on time to pay them.

Now, as we have already learned, if a company does not make a profit-- if it is "losing" money, it is in big trouble. Sure enough. If revenues are less than those costs in a certain year, they don't make enough money to pay all those bills. What does a company do in this case? Well, most companies keep some cash on hand, kind of a rainy day fund. They can use that. But what do they do if that runs out? They can try to borrow money. But that will cover them only for a while, until the lenders suspect they are in trouble. After that, they can try to sell off parts of their business. But that takes a lot of time. So usually, if a company is still in trouble, they end up in Chapter 11 bankruptcy. If that doesn't work out, they go out of business completely. All the remaining employees lose their jobs. All the equipment is sold, and the proceeds are used to pay off part of the company's loans. Stockholders end up with nothing. That's called Chapter 7 bankruptcy. End of the line.

How often does this happen? Every year, some well-known companies go into Chapter 11 bankruptcy. Ever heard of K-Mart, US Airways, United Airlines, Enron, WorldCom, Global Crossing, LTV Steel? They all went into bankruptcy recently. Continental Airlines went through bankruptcy some years ago, and is surviving quite well. Eastern Airlines and Pan American Airlines, unfortunately didn't make it, and they no longer exist.

The message here is that making money and surviving is not always easy for a corporation. But how do they actually get into trouble, in the first place? And once they are in trouble, how do they get out of it?

Let's look first at how they get into financial trouble. There are usually two ways. One way is to make bad investments. The other way is to become uncompetitive. We'll look at both. Let's start with bad investments.

Do you remember that company that decided to build a new factory? They decided to do it because they thought they could sell a lot more of the products that they make. In order to build the new factory, they had to borrow a lot of money. Now, let's assume that they were wrong about how much new product they would sell. For example, they didn't do a good job studying and researching the market for their products. Or, maybe another company, a competitor, made the decision to build a big factory at the same time. In either case, the new factory is not being used much.

Regardless, the company still has to pay all the employees, all the insurance and maintenance costs, and all the yearly loan costs for that new factory. These costs don't change a whole lot, whether the factory is producing 40 % of capacity, or 100 % of capacity. Economists call them "fixed costs", because they don't change much as production varies up or down.

If the new factory is only making, say, 40 % of its maximum capacity, generally it will be losing money. The revenues from product sales will be less than the costs to run the factory. This could be big trouble. It depends how big the company is. If other company operations are making enough money to cover the losses from the new factory, the company is still okay. It still makes a profit. However, the total company profit is less than it was before the new factory was built. That could make the owners of the company-- the stock holders --hopping mad at the company's top managers--those guys who made the decision to build the factory in the first place.

Maybe being the chief executive of a company, the top boss, is not so great after all! Actually, a lot of these guys have been fired lately, either because their companies went into bankruptcy, or because the companies' profits have fallen a lot. Those highly-paid company managers can lose their jobs if they have make bad investment decisions. It is, in fact, a common occurrence.

Okay, let's consider now the other way a company can get into financial trouble-- by becoming uncompetitive. This often happens if a company's costs get too high, compared to the competition. If you are a company making cars, for example, and your profit margin is 5 %, your revenues are 5% higher than your costs. That's good, right? Now, what happens if your managers are not so good, and the profit margin sinks to zero? You are in trouble. How does that happen? Well, you have a bunch of other car companies, and they are always coming up with ideas to reduce costs, in order to increase profits. They all do it. Then they think, "Hmm, if I reduce my car prices, I can sell more cars, but still make a profit." A company with really good management will finally make that decision, when their profit margins are fat enough. Now, if your management is not good at reducing costs, you might end up being forced to reduce prices to the point that your profit margin has disappeared. You are now in big trouble. Usually what happens in this case is that the top manager gets fired, and the company tries to find someone who can fix the situation. If that effort is successful, it usually involves reducing manpower (i.e., firing people again), and perhaps reducing wages and salaries.

This is exactly what happened to United Airlines in 2002. United Airlines went into Chapter 11 bankruptcy, and has renegotiated all of the contracts it had made with the unions that represent its employees. As it turns out, United's pilots, maintenance workers, and other employees had much higher wages and salaries than the same types of employees at some other airlines, such as Southwest Airlines and Jet Blue. United had become UNCOMPETITIVE. The top boss lost his job, and many other people followed.

There is another way for a company to become uncompetitive. This happens when companies are making or selling products that people (consumers) don't want. Who would buy a pair of bell-bottomed, checked, polyester slacks? Nobody would now, but they sure were popular in the 1970's, believe it or not! How about a car that breaks down a lot, has big, ugly tail fins, and consumes loads of gasoline? Nobody now, but they sure were popular in the 1960's. Who would buy a mechanical calculator that costs over a $100, and that you have to crank to get an answer? Nobody now, but they were used everywhere in the 1950's. Who would want to fly from New York to Los Angeles on a noisy, slow, propeller-driven plane, and pay several thousand dollars for it? Nobody now, but that was the only way to do it in the 1950's and early 1960's.

Things like cars, airplanes, and clothes get better every year. What causes that? COMPETITION. Corporations put a lot of money every year into research and development. They spend this money to improve their existing products, and to develop new products. If they don't do it well, they will eventually die. Like Studebaker Corp., which used to make cars. Like Wang Corp., which used to make computers.

You are walking around with a cell phone, acting as if it's the most natural thing in the world. Thirty years ago, it was science fiction! I have a gas furnace in my house that is 95 % efficient (only 5 % of the energy from the fuel burned is lost to the atmosphere). Twenty years ago, the best furnace was about only 75% efficient. I could go on and on with examples. All these wonderful new products and improvements were caused by COMPETITION--corporations striving to make more money by making better goods and services.

Now an important question comes to mind. What is an economy like that doesn't have competition, that doesn't have loads of corporations competing with each other? The answer is a socialist or a communist economy. We talked about these economies briefly earlier in the book. The government is in charge of all the companies. There is no competition because there is basically only one shoe company, one car company, and so on. With no competition, there is no incentive to improve your products or develop new ones. There is no incentive to drive costs down. The result is a bunch of lousy products. Shoes that are ugly and don't fit well. Cars that are ugly, noisy, smelly, and break down a lot.

With no incentive to reduce costs, every company and every farm has way too many people, who also don't work very hard. The workday seems extremely long and boring. Factory and farm equipment is unreliable and breaks down a lot. People don't get much money, because they don't produce much. To make ends meet, you might have to hold down two jobs. The result is that everyone is poor, and you have to get into long lines to buy many things, like decent meat.

So, now you see the difference. Do you like our rough-and-tumble, free enterprise system, with its highly-competitive, cut-throat corporations?. Or do you prefer the socialist/communist system, where everyone wears the same ugly clothes, eats the same lousy food, drives the same awful little stinky cars, where you can't improve your standard of living much, no matter how hard you try. I think most of you would agree that our system is better. That doesn't say that we couldn't make it better than it is. It could be better, and it must become better. We will discuss some ways to do so in the following chapters.

Chapter 5. Government and the Economy

Everyone complains about the government, and businessmen are no exception. Taxes are too high. Too many regulations. If the president is a democrat, businessmen might complain that he is too cosy with the labor unions. Oh, no, the government has raised the minimum wage again! That is bad for business. How can we compete with foreign businesses? We need import duties or quotas because those foreign companies are dumping cheap products into our country. They will drive us out of business! Blah, blah, it goes on and on.

Then you have environmental groups, complaining that the government is too soft on business. Those power plants in the Midwest are belching out tons of sulfur dioxide every hour, which are poisoning the air and lakes in upstate New York and New England. Those bloody oil companies want to drill for oil in Alaska, in a wildlife refuge, of all places. They must be stopped! How about those cigarette companies, whose products are poisoning helpless teenagers and killing nicotine-addicted adults. Why doesn't the government do something!!??

If you get the idea that government is an important player in the economy, you are so right. As money is the bloodstream of the economy, and corporations are the vital organs of the economy, government is both the central nervous system and conscience of the economy. It is extremely important that you understand this.

Good government can make an economy grow and prosper while protecting the health and well-being of its citizens. Bad government can cripple an economy, and make its citizens unhealthy, poor, and unsafe.

Government provides the critical leadership that can make a nation great or a deplorable basket case.

People are born essentially the same, wherever they live. The environment that they grow up in is largely determined by the effectiveness of their government. If you were born in Zimbabwe or Somalia, you would be poor, hungry, and dirty like most of the people there. Zimbabwe has a rotten government, while Somalia has essentially no government. As any recent immigrant to the US would readily tell you, you are indeed fortunate to be living in this country, which has a long history of good, effective government. You got that? Good.

How can we be sure that it will stay good? You have to recognize that there are tremendous pressures on our elected officials from so-called "special interests". These are groups or organizations that want the government to change laws or regulations to suit their purposes. It might be steel companies asking for import duties (taxes) on imported steel, because they can't compete with the price of the imports. This would be good for the steel makers and their employees, but it would not good for the average consumer, who must then pay higher prices for all products that contain steel, such as cars, refrigerators, washing machines, etc..

It might be farmers in the Midwest pushing for adding ethanol into gasoline. It's good for them, because it provides another market for their corn (ethanol, or drinking alcohol, is made in this case from fermenting corn). However, it is not good for the average consumer in the US because it raises the cost of gasoline.

Sometimes labor unions pressure our elected officials to raise the minimum wage. This benefits some people who are working in minimum wage jobs, and it makes the sponsors of such legislation look good, but it can have some bad effects. It can push up the prices of certain goods, because companies will try to raise prices to cover their increased costs and maintain their profit margins. Also, some companies will lay off some lower paid employees, or stop hiring them. Virtually all economists think it is better for the free market to set wages, not the government, but we have a minimum wage law nonetheless.

As you can see, government influence and control is a very complicated issue. Most officials in our government want to do the right thing, but they are under a lot of pressure much of the time to do the wrong thing. Sometimes they are not sure what is right or wrong. The minimum wage issue is good for some people, but not good for others. The same applies with regard to ethanol in gasoline. If you are a senator from a farm state, you would probably vote for ethanol in gasoline. It benefits some influential people in your state, but it is bad for most Americans. If you are a senator from New England, you would probably vote against ethanol, because nobody much grows corn in your state. Your vote would benefit most Americans.

That's the way things work in our form of government. But you know what? Usually (and I emphasize--usually), things come out best for the majority of the American people. Some things slip through, such as ethanol in gasoline. However, generally, our elected officials do the right thing when acting as a group, even when each one is voting as a special interest advocate. Why? Well, to get a bill passed in Congress, a majority of congressmen and senators have to vote yes. Furthermore, for a congressional bill to become a law, the President has to vote yes, also, by signing the bill into law.

Okay, let's get back to what government should be doing in the marketplace, in the economy. As we found in the last chapter, the key players in the economy are companies and corporations. What determines their behavior? Their main goals are to make the largest profit possible and to be a top competitor. However, they have to obey certain laws and regulations created and enforced by local, state, and federal governments. Companies are in a competitive game, and those laws and regulations are the rules of the game. And we certainly need those rules, because corporations play rough. You will remember that a corporation has to make a profit to survive, and a manager can lose his job if his part of the business doesn't make enough of a profit. As a result, a corporation will try to play to the limit of the rules, and sometimes try to stretch them.

What kind of rules are we talking about? There are a lot of rules. Primarily they are about pollution, competitive practices, corruption, and labor practices. As an example, let's talk about pollution. A lot of companies produce pollution along with their products--air pollution, water pollution, and pollution of the earth. In the earlier days in this country, pollution was a big problem. Progressively tougher regulations have solved most of the problem. In most countries, however, pollution is still a big problem.

In the early 1990's, I visited an oil refinery in Argentina, and it was a real mess. There was so much oil leaking from the refinery that the downstream waterways had loads of oil on their banks. So much oil in fact that the oil would sometimes catch on fire and endanger nearby homes. Even when the oil was not on fire, it was bad for the local residents because of the unhealthy fumes and bad smell coming from the spilt oil. The government of Argentina has enforced cleanup of that mess, in the meantime. Thank goodness! But how does that actually work?

In cases like oil refineries, the government imposes emission controls on how much oil can escape into the waterways. It also imposes controls on air pollutants as well, such as sulfur dioxide and oil fumes. In order to do this right, a government has to know what technology is available for cleaning up the emissions. If the rules are too strict and expensive, the company might decide to close the oil refinery and make oil products elsewhere. If that happens, all the employees would lose their jobs, which would be a disaster for them and the local economy.

As you can see, the rules imposed on a company have to be strict, yet reasonable. They have to take into account what technology is available, and what effect the rules might have on the COMPETITIVENESS of the company. There's that word again! Every time we talk about the economy, local or national, we have to consider competitiveness.

For example, if we impose very strict emission rules on our steel plants, the cost of making the steel might become so high that they could not compete with steel imported from other countries, where emission rules are not as strict. A good government is always considering such issues when making up rules for local businesses. It has to balance the desire for a clean environment with the hard economic realities of the marketplace.

Fortunately, as time goes on, the technology for pollution control gets better and better, so the air and water in our country have become much cleaner. Why does it get better? Because of COMPETITION among the companies that produce and use pollution control equipment. They do it better and cheaper year after year. For example, the automobiles of the 1960's were quite dirty, belching out unburned fuel and oil, and lead! Today's cars emit only a few percent of that amount of unburned fuel and oil, and no lead. Also they produce only a small percent of the amounts of sulfur dioxide and nitrogen oxides, which overall has greatly reduced air pollution, particularly in big cities.

It is worth mentioning that today's cars are also much more reliable, and breakdowns on the road are quite rare, compared to the 1960's. All of this was made possible by cooperation among the car companies, oil companies, and technology companies promoted by the steady, guiding hand of good government.

It is important to focus right now on one more area where good government rules are important-- MAINTAINING competition among companies. We have certain laws and certain policies in effect to prevent any corporation or small group of companies from getting too much power. In the beginning of the 20th century, President Teddy Roosevelt kicked off this "anti-trust" policy by breaking up the Standard Oil Trust. This was a large company, headed by John D. Rockefeller, which dominated the oil industry in the US. That large company became several smaller ones, which you might readily recognize. Exxon, Mobil, Texaco, Chevron, Amoco are all offspring of that breakup. A similar breakup occurred in the steel industry.

A more recent example of government anti-trust action involves Microsoft Corporation which produces software for computers. A long court case ended recently, in which the US government sued Microsoft for anti-competitive behavior. Microsoft was ordered by the court to change certain policies and practices. These changes are expected to make life easier for Microsoft's competitors, and to benefit anyone who uses a computer. Those benefits would be (1) more and better software products to choose from, and (2) lower prices for them.

Okay, I hope you get the picture now. Good government is critically important for a healthy economy and a healthy environment. It has to have a good set of rules in place to promote competition among corporations and protect the environment. It also has to protect the shareholders of public companies from corrupt practices by company managers. That is why you see executives from Enron, WorldCom, Tyco, and Adelphia in court facing serious criminal charges.

What did they do wrong? They are charged with making false claims about their profits, i.e., overstating them, making false claims about the financial health of their companies, and in some cases, using company funds for their own private use.

But good government has even more work to do. In the next chapter, we will address the issue of taxation policy, and how it affects the health of the economy.

Chapter 6. Taxation Policy

Okay, you say there is no way that a discussion on taxes could be interesting, right? Well, what are your biggest deductions on your paycheck? Taxes. Federal income taxes, social security taxes (FICA), Medicare taxes, state taxes. If you don't care about these things, you could skip this chapter. Wait a minute! Did you know that when you buy gasoline, forty some cents per gallon goes to state and federal excise taxes? When you buy clothing or other things in a store, you might be paying 6-8% sales tax? When you buy your first house, you'll be paying out a large chunk of property taxes that could be several thousand dollars a year or more? When you buy ANYTHING, you are paying a hidden tax---the corporate income tax? What, how is that possible? The corporations have already paid that tax, right? That's right, but they pass ALL of it on to you. It's included in the price of their products. They have to do that, in order to make a profit.

So, if you don't learn anything else in this chapter, you will learn one thing. Whenever some idiot appears on television and advocates higher corporate taxes to "soak the rich" you will know he is an idiot. Let's go over this in a little more detail. The lower the income level of a person, the higher the percentage of his income is used to buy things--food clothing, shelter, etc.--often 100%. Most of this stuff is made by corporations. Rich people, by contrast, save a large percent of their incomes, and spend only a part of it. So already the rich are paying less corporate income tax per dollar of income than a middle class person. Also, the rich are a small percentage of our population. Most goods and services produced by corporations are bought by middle and lower class Americans. So, again, they are bearing the burden of the "hidden" corporate income taxes, not the rich.

Still don't care about taxes? Unless you're brain-dead, I'll bet you do care, so read on!

Okay, what is the purpose of taxes? Broadly speaking, there are two purposes: (1) to pay for the operations of federal, state, and local governments, and (2) to cover the costs of transfer payments. What? What are transfer payments? These are transfers of money from your pocket to someone else's. We've discussed most of them already, but under another name--entitlements. Examples are social security, Medicare, Medicaid, welfare, farm subsidies, veterans' benefits. I'm sure there are others, but these are the ones that come to mind right off. Transfer payments are the biggest part of the federal budget--two thirds, in fact--much bigger, for example than the defense budget.

The second thing to address is who pays the taxes, and who should pay the taxes? Consumers pay the taxes--people. Just people! What? Yes, yes, corporations pay taxes, but as we already discussed, they pass them all on to you--every dollar. You really have to get over this mindset that corporations are somehow "rich people". They are not people!! So stop it.

Okay, now you agree that ultimately, at the end of the day, only people pay taxes. So, which people? Actually, in this country we do have a policy that rich people should pay a higher tax on income than poor people. You can readily see that by looking at the tax tables on your federal income tax instruction form. As your income goes higher and higher, your additional income falls into higher and higher tax brackets, with a maximum of some 35%. If you are really rich, you might have to pay an additional tax called the "Alternative Minimum Tax" (AMT).

If you look at that same form you can see that very poor people who work can actually "pay" a negative income tax, if they have one or more children. These people, in effect, can get an income tax refund that is larger than the total taxes that were deducted from their income during the year. By total taxes, I mean federal income tax plus FICA plus Medicare. By the way, this special tax payback is called the "earned income tax credit". If you are poor, but earn some income, you can get a tax credit. This policy provides some help and incentive to the working poor, which is good.

This method of taxation is called "progressive", which means the more money you make, the higher your percent tax on total income. Progressive taxation is common economic policy in all developed countries. In European countries, it is carried to an extreme with incremental rates as high as 50% or more. It used to be that way in the US, but our government decided that such high taxation levels stifled economic growth. In fact, President Bush has recently succeeded in lowering our maximum rate somewhat more (from 38.6 to 35%). More about that later.

Anyhow, the opposite of "progressive" is "regressive". Any regressive taxes that exist hit the lower income levels harder than the higher ones. Examples of regressive taxes are sales taxes and excise taxes. That's because lower-income people spend more of their earnings than rich people do. Also, the rich people are a very small percent of the population, and the lower and middle classes thus do most of the spending. Sound familiar? Yes, just like the corporate income tax we discussed above. Therefore we can also call the corporate income tax a regressive tax as well.

At this point you should realize that our tax policy is inconsistent. We have some taxes that are progressive and some are regressive. That does not make sense. Also, we should point out that our income tax laws are extremely complicated. Because of those complications, we have a total industry of people --accountants and lawyers-- who provide tax advice to corporations and individuals. These people are well educated, extremely bright, and they make loads of money. But they produce nothing. Not one ounce of useful goods or services. Can you imagine how much we could boost the productivity of this country by simplifying the tax code, and putting these people into productive jobs? Oh, boy. Let me tell you that this is the one area where our government has really screwed up. It has resulted from decades of congressmen relentlessly tinkering with the tax code. It is so bad that the time has come for all good Americans to demand a total overhaul. Since the time has come, and I happen to be writing a book, why don't I take a first shot at it? Let's get moving!

Okay, first of all, a rational tax code needs some basic principles that should be clear and fair. Let's write them down right now.

(1) Taxes should be progressive. Your tax rate should go up progressively with your income.

(2) Taxes should be simple, direct, and transparent. You should be aware of every tax that you pay and why.

(3) Tax policy, and indeed every government policy, should be formulated to promote the productivity of our work force and economy.

That's it. With those principles in mind, let's set up the basic structure of a new, simple, and fair tax code.

(1) Abolish the corporate income tax. It violates all three of the principles established above. It is regressive, it is hidden and indirect, and it has created hoards of accountants and lawyers who make big salaries, but produce nothing for the economy. Let's put those people to work doing something useful. That was easy, huh?.

(2) Replace the lost revenues from abolishing the corporate income tax by imposing a new progressive federal sales tax. I don't have the time, expertise, or data to propose anything exact, but it should be roughly as follows. For small, but critical items, such as food and clothing, it should be a very small percentage. As items get costlier, the tax rate should go up. When you finally get up to luxury cars and boats, the rate should be the highest. In order to keep things simple, I would suggest that there be maybe ten categories and ten corresponding tax rates. At the low end, for individual items up to $20, the tax rate could be 1 % or lower. At the high end, for items over $50,000, the tax rate could be 5%, or whatever. A special tax could also be imposed for luxury homes--those over $500,000 or so. These federal sales taxes would be in addition to the local and state sales taxes already imposed on goods and services.

Now, don't start complaining about new taxes! All of these new taxes will be offset by lower prices for goods and services. What? How is that possible? Don't forget that under this plan, corporations can now reduce their prices while maintaining their profit margins because they no longer have to pay taxes. Also, they will be able to reduce their prices even further because they can cut costs by getting rid of a lot of expensive accountants and lawyers! A further benefit to all such companies is that they will be more price-competitive on exporting goods and services to other countries. When you look at everything, the total price of an average item, including tax, should be somewhat lower. Isn't that great? Why didn't someone think of this earlier? I don't know. Let's go on.

What? You see a potential problem? Ahh, good thinking! You are suggesting that the rich can avoid the high sales taxes on expensive items by leasing (renting) them instead of buying them. Yes, they would try to do that, wouldn't they. They're a bloody clever lot! Okay, in that case, when they lease an expensive item, they should pay the sales tax up front, as if they had paid the full purchase price. Alternatively, if you want to give them a bit of a break, you could split up that same tax over the years of the lease--as long as the lease isn't too long. Let's go on.

(3) Simplify the federal income tax code by eliminating almost all personal deductions. Okay, if you want to promote home ownership, let's keep the deduction for home mortgage interest. You might want to maintain deductions for massive medical bills and child day care expenses for the working poor, but that's it! As far as charitable contributions are concerned, I feel they are a totally personal decision and responsibility. I don't like the idea, as a taxpayer, of paying a 35 % share of some rich guy's charitable contribution. He should do it all himself. I believe that the American people are kind and generous, and they don't need the government involved in their decisions on charity.

(4) Get rid of special treatment for capital gains profits. Right now, if you own some stock for more than a year, and you sell it for a profit, your maximum tax rate on the profit is only 15%, versus 35 % for "normal" income. Since most people buying and selling stock are well-to-do, why in heaven's name are we allowing them a bargain basement tax rate? This is clearly a regressive tax. Get rid of it!

(5) Get rid of FICA and Medicare taxes. These are regressive taxes--a fixed percent of each dollar earned. Even worse, they are deducted from after-tax income, so they are double taxation. Worse still, the FICA tax is extracted only up to a certain fixed income level. Any income above that is not taxed. How's that for a brutally regressive tax?

(6) Maintain the current progressive tax rate structure for federal personal income taxes. Adjust all the tax rates to account for the loss of income from FICA and Medicare taxes. Be careful, however that we do not increase them too much at the upper end. Why? Because high tax rates lead to bad behavior. For example, back when the maximum rate was 70%, there was little incentive to work harder and make more money. That is bad because our most productive citizens are usually the highest-paid ones. Also, at ultra-high tax rates, there is a much larger incentive to cheat on taxes, particularly among small businessmen, by not reporting income or overstating costs. The temptation is just too great.

In order to avoid ultra-high income tax rates, it would be better to adjust upward the higher levels of the proposed progressive sales tax (point 2 above). That would encourage rich people to buy less and invest more. What a deal for the rest of us!

(7) Get rid of the estate tax. A law to do so is already on the books, with progressive phase-out over a ten-year period. However, according to that same law, it could be completely re-instated at the end of the ten year period. Let's not do that. Look, under the tax plan outlined above, we're soaking the rich pretty good on their annual income. It is unfair to give them a final wallop on their deathbeds. If they managed to raise and keep a lot of money during their lives, in spite of our progressive taxation, let them keep it, for heaven's sake. Since when is it American to swoop in on a family and take away one third to one half of their assets? It is also damaging to the economy, because most of these "rich" people are small business owners and farmers. Those businesses could be ruined or weakened by the government demanding a large chunk of the family assets. Don't forget that these are the businesses that provide the most new jobs in the economy.

That's all that I have to offer in this chapter. Wasn't it fun? Hey, one other thing I should mention here. Last year (2003), the Bush administration proposed and passed into law major tax cuts to stimulate the economy. One main expensive item was to reduce the so-called double taxation of corporate dividends. Corporations pay income taxes and then pay dividends to shareholders from their after-tax profits. Individuals who receive such dividends then have to pay federal income tax on those dividends. That's double taxation. The new law reduces the tax paid by those individuals on dividends to 15%. These individuals are mainly wealthy. This is clearly regressive, a no-no. Wait, I'm not finished! Also passed into law was a reduction in capital gains tax, from 20 to 15%. Who pays capital gains taxes? Mainly the rich, as mentioned earlier. So, you now have the following situation. A rich person who doesn't work, and lives off stocks and bonds has a pretty sweet deal. He, or she, can live off interest from tax-free municipal bonds, plus any capital gains from selling stocks and bonds, taxed at only 15%, plus dividends, which are taxed at only 15%! Of course, there is something called the alternative minimum tax (AMT) in the federal tax code, which might capture an additional tax bite from that person. However, overall, the recent Bush tax cuts are clearly favoring the rich over the middle class and the poor, and are clearly regressive.

Whoa! One more issue should be addressed. You all have heard of Rush Limbaugh, the conservative radio talk show host? Sure. Well, in support of the Bush tax cuts, he has claimed recently that low-income folks should not get any tax relief. Why? Because they pay little or no income tax. He is right about that. However, he is dead wrong that they should get no tax relief versus the rich. Why? As we have already discussed, the low-income folks pay a lot of taxes in the form of payroll taxes (FICA plus Medicare), corporate income tax, excise taxes, sales taxes, and property taxes. Regardless what label we put on these taxes, they are simply taxes. Also, in total, they are a large percent of a low-income person's income. And they are a large percentage of a middle-income person's income. These people need tax relief the most. But who got the most from the Bush tax cuts? The rich. Come on, Democrats, where is your outrage, for heaven's sake?

Chapter 7. Social Security, Medicare, and Economic Growth.

When I was your age, I did not care much about social security or Medicare. It was just an annoyingly large deduction from my paycheck. I was aware, however, that by paying those deductions, I would be entitled to social security and Medicare when I retired. Now at age 61, I am looking forward to getting my first social security check by the end of this year. After all, I earned it, right? I paid FICA and Medicare for years and years. Some of my political leaders have assured me that money went into the "Social Security Trust Fund". Or a "Lockbox", as often verbalized by Al Gore or the former Senate majority leader, Trent Lott.

Let's get something straight, right off. Social security is a pay-as-you-go system. What do I mean by that? As described in the last chapter, it is a transfer payment that goes from your pocket to a retiree's pocket via the federal government. If you are an eligible retiree, you earned an entitlement to that money by faithfully paying into FICA and Medicare during your working years. It's all straight-forward and legal.

So where is the fiction? There is a false impression created by the use of words like "Trust Fund" and "Lock Box" that your paycheck deductions are going into a special fund or bank, and being kept there safe and sound. It's not being used for other purposes, and certainly not for wasteful purposes. That's the fiction.

Here's how it works. It's a bit of a shell game by the federal government. The government rakes in two types of tax revenues: (1) general revenues, which come from income taxes and excise (sales) taxes, and (2) social taxes, which are the payroll deductions for FICA and Medicare. The social taxes go temporarily into those fictional funds called "Trust Funds". Money is then deducted from those funds to pay retirees. If there is something left over, it is LOANED to the federal government in the form of bonds. That money then flows into the general revenues stream, and is used to pay other federal government bills and obligations--fighter planes, tanks, ammunition, salaries of elected officials and government employees, farm subsidies, interest on the federal debt, various pork barrel projects, etc.

Now stop right there. What?! A part of the US government, the social security administration, lends money to the US government. The government is lending money to itself?? That implies that later on, the US government will have to pay itself back. Ha, ha, sounds a little crazy, no? It is. Anyhow let's go on.

If there is not enough money collected from FICA and Medicare payroll deductions to pay all the social security and Medicare bills, money is taken from the general revenues stream to make up the difference. What? Where the hell else would you get it? From the The Trust Fund? I told you, there is no piggy bank!! Okay, calm down. Finish the story. In this case, if the social security administration has those US government bonds from previous surplus years, it will "cash them in" to cover what it has taken from the general revenue stream.

If there are no bonds left, nothing really changes. You will still get your social security and Medicare entitlements covered if you are a retiree. The government will continue dipping into general revenues, and go into deficit spending, if necessary. If the government refuses to pay up in full, you can be sure that the old folks will vote as a block in the next election to kick out those responsible. So forget it, it won't happen.

I think you're getting the picture, but let's summarize it carefully. The government will make social security and Medicare payments for those who have entitlements. The total amount paid out every year is really a political decision. It has nothing to do with fictional trust funds. The entitlements paid have to be enough to appear fair to the recipients--those who faithfully paid payroll taxes all those years that they worked. However, it cannot be so much that the current work force, which is providing all the funds, is overburdened with high taxes. That's the whole story.

How in the world did all this happen in the first place? Let's give you some quick historical perspective. Back in the 1930's, times were very hard, there was a major economic depression. A lot of old folks were poverty-stricken. As part of his overall plan to revive the economy, and take care of the poor, Franklin Roosevelt established, with the necessary concurrence of the Congress, the Social Security Administration. His aim was merely to make sure that old folks would always have some money coming in, so they wouldn't be destitute. And he was sure they would spend every bit of it, which would stimulate the economy. To prevent it from looking like a simple hand-out at the time (which it was), he put the taxes into a special category. In order to make it acceptable to active workers, he made it a type of insurance plan. You pay in now, and you'll get the money back when you are retired. Kind of like forced savings. Except that the money you put in now would not go into some piggy bank, it would be immediately spent by someone else.

Now this kind of a scheme will work well forever, so long as you don't get too generous, and new workers keep popping up (or out) at the required rate to pay the bills. Well, with the onset of significant inflation, some decades ago, the government began to index social security payments to the inflation rate. So the payments started going up every year. Then they decided further that old folks need not only social security monthly payments, but also some help with medical bills. So they created Medicare, and another fictitious "trust fund" to go with it. Hell, social security worked so well, why break the mold?

Well, as if that weren't enough to make you a bit edgy, during the same time frame, birth rates in the US plummeted due to the advent of birth control pills. And then came legal abortion to make it worse. All of those little guys and gals who could have become new workers--they never showed up! And to make matters worse, people have been living longer due to better working conditions, cleaner environment, and modern medicine.

As a result of these trends, Congress has started a practice of jacking up social security and Medicare deductions from our paychecks. It could be worse, but thank goodness for productivity improvements in our economy, it's not so bad--so far.

Looking down the road, it looks worse. We're still not having enough kids, and the number of old folks is increasing fast, especially with the coming retirement of the so-called baby boomers. Those are the geezers who were born during the sexual frenzy following World War II.

The government now estimates that the social security trust fund, which now has an annual surplus, will become break-even around 2017, and Medicare even sooner. After that they will have to start "cashing in" those ridiculous, worthless, fictitious bonds. Finally, by 2041 or so, the bonds will even run out. What are we to do? Well, do what you've done before. Create a high level commission to study the situation for a year or two. Then you do what you've done before, and raise payroll deductions again. You might ease the load on workers somewhat by cutting back a bit on the inflation index on social security payments, and raising the official retirement age. Hurrah, we're saved again!

Okay, now I'm really mad. I'll tell you why. If the government does this exercise soon, as seems likely to be the case, the social security surpluses will go up. As discussed earlier, those surpluses do not go into some goddam piggy bank, they go into the general revenues stream, where they will be SPENDABLE. Of course, they could be used to reduce the federal debt, but that is not the historical practice. Congress always finds some way to spend the money. They could use some of the money for a pet project in Congressman Pork's district, or they could increase farm subsidy payments to already rich farmers. What, you thought only poor farmers got subsidies!? Boy, are you misinformed. But not any more, because you took the time to read this lovely little book.

Okay now, you have two choices. You can do Plan A and go with the president's commission on social security and Medicaid. Or you can go with Plan B. My plan. Interested? I'll assume you said yes. Here it is.

-Immediately abolish the federal deductions on payroll checks for social security and Medicare. As I indicated previously, these are brutally regressive taxes and should be abolished. The other reason is to reduce future federal taxes and expenditures. What? How? By abolishing social taxes, you abolish the social security and Medicare surpluses, which are being spent happily by Congress. You remember that presidential commission? It was going to increase your payroll taxes and thus the social security surplus. Now they can't do it, not in Plan B.

-Fund social security and Medicare (SS&M) from general revenues. Set a target for SS&M payouts as a fixed percent of the average worker's paycheck and stick to it. In other words, the total payout to retirees would be the fixed percent of total wages and salaries earned by the workforce. Adjust payments to individual retirees yearly as required, and inform people well ahead of time on any changes. In other words, bite the bullet. You could make things easier for the poorer retirees by taxing the social security payments to the richer ones, and giving that tax amount to the poorer ones.

-As mentioned earlier, compensate for the loss of SS&M tax deductions by adjusting the rates on the progressive income tax and the new progressive national sales tax.

That's it, that's Plan B.

At this point, you might say, hey, what about those private savings accounts the Bushies have been talking about? Their idea is to take part of your monthly social security contribution, say 10%, and putting it into a special savings account. The money there could be used to buy a mixture of things like stocks, bonds, CD's, whatever. That 10% will no longer be part of the current social security surplus, and Congressman Pork will not be able to do his project. Or we might have to cut back on those farm subsidy payments to rich farmers. What a shame.

My position on the Bush plan is mildly favorable, but only if the current system remains in effect. The Bush plan takes away much of the social security surplus from the politicians, and hopefully gets them to reduce non-essential spending. That's essentially the goal. However, if they don't reduce such spending, our federal deficit will go up, which is bad.

The better way to go is to abolish the tax deductions for social security and Medicare, as outlined earlier. This action gets rid of the social security and Medicare surpluses immediately and totally, and the incentive for congressmen to spend them.

Also, I firmly believe that social security should remain a defined entitlement. That money should always be there, however little it might be. However badly you might have managed your other assets, social security is still there.. Forget those private accounts.

After all this enlightening discussion, you probably forgot the title of this chapter. I'll remind you that the last part was "Economic Growth". What does that have to do with anything here? A lot. Let's go back to Chapter 1 and that little equation that we had developed:

Economic Output = Number of Workers x Average Worker Productivity

If we get the right number of workers and their productivity up to the right level, we can handle any number of retirees. That's basically what the equation promises. Make the economic pie big enough, and everyone gets an acceptable share. So how do we do that? Why not set up a presidential commission to study it? Aw, come on, stop it. Hey, we can use the same guys we just kicked off the presidential commission for social security. At least they'll be working on something that makes sense. Okay, let's do it! But what if they just talk a lot and don't have any ideas? Hmm, that could be a problem. All right, let's give them some ideas to start with. Here goes.

With regard to the number of workers, we either have to have more kids, or more immigrants. If our young adults are going to continue their practice of low productivity in this area, we have to bring in more immigrants. Actually, we are already doing just that. The number of US residents who were not born here is above 10% of the population. It hasn't been that high since the early 1900's. That's good... I guess. But you keep reading that immigrants are a big drain on our social services and schools. We need ESL, and so on to educate them. Wait! On the other hand, the metropolitan areas that have lots of immigrants are booming—e. g.,, LA, New York, Washington, Chicago. And those that don't are not--Cleveland, Detroit, to name a few. In fact, Pittsburgh, Pa. last year announced a policy to attract immigrants to their lovely town on the banks of Allegheny, Monongahela, and Ohio rivers. I guess immigrants are good. Of course, they're good. We have been bringing them in for years, right from our earliest days as a republic. Immigrants are good, and we're good at Americanizing them. Let's keep up the good work. But let's scrutinize them, and keep them under control so that we do not have another 9/11/2001.

Having solved the worker number problem, how do we improve productivity? Now here is an area that we Americans have been particularly successful in recent years. If you go back to that neat little chart in Chapter 2, we will generate some ideas.

First of all, how do you improve the so-called productivity boosters--plant and equipment, infrastructure, and raw material extraction? By expanding them, and modernizing them. That takes money. Where does it come from? In the case of infrastructure, it comes primarily from taxes and loans. That's mainly government project work. In the case of private plant, equipment, and raw material extraction, the money comes from company profits, new stock, and loans. Where does the money for new stock and loans come from? From people saving money. They put the money into savings accounts, CD's, and bonds, or buy the new stocks. Who are these people? Rich people, people who don't spend everything they earn.

So rich people can be good! Yup, in our system they can be useful. They are essential. And if you get yourself educated, and work hard, you can become one of them. It happens all the time. There is one other thing about rich people that you should know. They not only have money, most of them are quite smart. That means they will try to put their money into the best investments, into the projects that will pay out the most money. Generally speaking, those are the projects that give the best productivity boosts to our economic system. Isn't our economic system great? Yes, it is. Just make sure that you continue to allow the opportunity for people to get rich, and make good investment decisions. In other words, don't tax the dickens out of them. Don't kill the golden goose.

Okay, let's move further to the right on that neat little diagram in Chapter 2. (I told you it would be useful. It helps you focus on the important concepts.) Let's look at those so-called productive organizations--private industry and government. What can they do to improve things? Let's give them three general rules:

(1) Promote good education and training for workers. It increases their productivity.

You think we do a good job already? Did you know that 37 % of the adults in our nation's capital, Washington, DC, read at the third grade level or lower? How productive are those people? Get serious. Overall, we are doing well, but we can do much better.

(2) Every worker should be in a job that promotes production or output in the economy.

Do you remember all those accountants and lawyers who help people and companies deal with our complex tax code? They all have to go. Not really, but they do have to take up new work, new productive jobs. But we need to install a simple tax code system first, and get rid of corporate incomes taxes.

(3) Make smart investments. Use your money well.

Why do we have government subsidies for rich farmers? Is that in the national interest? Why do we pay farmers to grow nothing on their land? Why do we have import quotas on sugar, so that our domestic price is three times the international market price? Why do the top bosses at big corporations get so much money and special favors? They are like pigs at a trough. As you can see, our leaders in government and business could use their money—our money-- more wisely. There is still plenty of room for improvement there.

That's it basically. (1)Good education and training for workers. (2)Get rid of stupid, wasteful jobs. (3)Spend our money wisely. So who should take the responsibility for doing all this? Mainly our government leaders and our leaders in private industry. That's their job! If you've got the stuff, become one of them. The rest of us can do something too. Write letters. Vote. Complain. Do volunteer political work. Demonstrate. Make contributions. Don't do nothing. If you've had the energy to read this book, you have the energy to do something. Be a good citizen. That's it for this chapter.

Chapter 8. Monetary and Fiscal Policy

Most normal folks would read the title of this chapter, and not have a clue what it means. The purpose of the chapter is to explain what it means, and why it is important. Have you ever heard, "We need tax cuts to stimulate the economy"? Have you ever heard "The Fed must use tight money to fight inflation"? Those are the types of things we are going to talk about here. Not in textbook language, but in everyday language that you can understand. Afterwards, when the president or a senator makes such statements, you will have a much better idea of what they are talking about, and whether they are making sense.

Let's talk about monetary policy first, because it involves money, which we all love. You will recall that money is the blood stream of our economy. Money is created by the Federal Reserve Bank (the "Fed"), which is a branch of the federal government. The amount of money in circulation at any given time is based on careful thinking and planning by the Board of Governors of the Fed to meet three important national goals:

-Money should remain valuable. That means that prices of goods and services should remain stable.

-Economic growth should be promoted.

-Low unemployment should be promoted.

These are good goals, but they are hard to achieve, and sometimes they conflict with one another. You want to know why? This takes some explanation, so read on.

Our wonderful economic system has one major flaw, or weakness. The economy tends to go in cycles. Sometimes we have booms, when economic growth rates are very high. These are usually followed by recessions, in which the economy actually declines. In booms, national output grows rapidly, whereas in recessions, national output goes down. But why does that happen?

During the boom periods, people and companies borrow a lot of money. They feel good. People buy a lot of things, and companies start building new factories, buildings, etc. to keep up with the demand. Unemployment is very low. Everything is dandy, except for one thing. Prices and wages go up very quickly. That's because the demand for goods and services have reached the capacity of the economic system to provide them. Remember that there is low unemployment, so there are no good people left on the bench, so to speak, to jump into the game. Labor unions recognize there is a labor shortage, so they threaten to go on strike unless they get high wage raises for their members. Since factories are operating at capacity, and making a lot of money, businessmen do not want a strike. Because their goods are in such high demand, they have the power to raise prices. So they go ahead and grant the wage increases. Then they increase prices in order to maintain their profit margins.

So what's bad about all that? Well, anybody that made a loan to someone else is very upset. He is getting paid back in dollars that are of less value than those he lent out. So the next time he makes a loan, he will charge a much higher interest rate. This goes on and on during a boom. Finally someone who wants to borrow money to buy a car says, "Hey wait a minute, I'm not sure I can afford the payments! Interest rates are so high, and I'm already deeply in debt." So he doesn't buy the car. Others start making the same decision. The next thing you know, companies see their profits start to go down, because they are selling less product. So what do they do? They start laying off people. Those people are now unable to buy very much, because they aren't making any money, and they must live off their savings until they find new jobs. At the same time, folks who still have jobs cut back their buying and save more money, because they are worried they will also lose their jobs. After a while, the boom is gone, and yikes, a recession has arrived!

This looks bad, and it is, for a while. But then, companies start offering special price deals on their merchandise or services. Since people are not borrowing much money anymore, banks start offering loans with low interest rates. This finally becomes very appealing to those folks who still have jobs.

They start buying more things, and eventually they start borrowing more money to buy those things. How about a new refrigerator, or a new car, or a new house? Then companies are making good money again. However, they find that they can't make enough product because they do not have enough employees. So they start to hire more people. Those people, who were formerly unemployed, now have money to buy things, and they do so. This behavior goes on until you have another boom, and the cycle starts all over again.

Okay, now you know all about booms and recessions. They are bad because the booms create inflation, and the recessions create unemployment. Our government recognizes that booms and recessions are a necessary evil of our economic system. Nevertheless, it seeks to find ways to flatten the peaks and fill in the troughs. The government's ultimate goals are to avoid excessive inflation during booms, and excessive unemployment rates during recessions.

How does it do that? Well, now we get back to the issue of monetary policy. When the Fed sees a boom coming on, it starts to tighten up the money supply--it starts taking money out of circulation. Borrowers have to compete harder to get loans, since there is less money around. Interest rates start to go up. People and businesses start postponing new loans, and this slows down their buying. As a result, the boom never arrives completely, and voila', we have avoided much of the bad effects of a boom--excessive price and wage inflation.

On the other side of the coin, when the Fed sees a slowdown occurring, it will loosen up on the money supply. Interest rates will go down, people will buy more, and there will be, at worst, a mild recession. Result: fewer losses of jobs.

In a nutshell, that is monetary policy. Some economists would say, "Oh no, it is much more complicated than that." I'm sure it is, but you have learned the bare essentials. Enough, already! Okay, now we are able to tackle fiscal policy.

Fiscal policy has exactly the same goals as monetary policy--low inflation and low unemployment. The levers of fiscal policy are different. They involve government actions on taxing and spending. For example, if we are approaching a boom, the federal government can increase taxes, take money out of peoples' pockets, and give to the Fed for safe keeping. Alternatively, it can cut back its own spending. Either action puts a damper on the growth of the economy.

During economic slowdowns, the government can do the exact opposite--reduce taxes and/or increase government spending. These actions stimulate economic growth. Reducing taxes is especially effective. First of all, normal folks get more money to spend and they do it right away. The rich people, on the other hand, put most of it into savings. As discussed earlier, this money finds its way into new investments for improving the productivity of the economy. A win-win situation.

That's it for fiscal policy. It can be used together with monetary policy to mitigate the effects of the business cycle.

There is one other related issue that we have to discuss before ending this chapter. I'm sure you have heard on the news a lot of yammering about government deficits and surpluses. All governments--local, state, and federal are either in deficit or surplus at any given time. Deficit means they are spending more than they are receiving in taxes. Surplus means the opposite.

Over time, local and state governments must balance their budgets, i.e., surpluses and deficits should balance out. That is the law in virtually all states. The federal government, however, is permitted to run deficits indefinitely, and it has done so over most of the last 50 years. How can it do so? Because it is allowed by law to do so. But if it is running deficits, where does it get the money to cover them? Only the federal government is able to create money--through the Federal Reserve Bank. If the federal government is in deficit, it can create money to cover the deficit. Alternatively, it can borrow money. This is getting interesting, right? Let's look at it a bit closer.

Creating money sounds so easy and so cool. Doesn't it? Well, there is one big problem. If you create too much money, the money loses its value. If you look at most developing countries, their money has lost enormous value over the years, because they created too much. I have a small collection of worthless, or near-worthless paper money from many such countries. Argentinian australes and pesos, Kenyan shillings, Russian rubles, Indonesian rupiahs, Nigerian naira and the list goes on, and on.

How about the US dollar? It also loses value over time, but at a much lower and acceptable rate. Why? Because the government has done a good job of creating new money to fit growing demand for it. Let's look at that a little closer.

First of all, as our economy grows, new money must be created. Otherwise, demand for it would push up interest rates, and that would slow down the growth of the economy. Secondly, the dollar is an international currency, so as the world economy grows, it needs more dollars as well. As a result, our government must continuously create new money to meet these two major demands.

Get the picture? Because of our large, growing economy, and the large, growing economy overseas, our government has to create money. In doing so, it can cover much of its deficits. What? How? Easy. The government creates the money, and then pays some bills with it. Once it does that, it has also fulfilled its obligation to increase money supply. Killing two birds with one stone.

Unfortunately, not all of its deficits can be covered this way. Why? Because excessive creation of money would destroy the value of the dollar, as discussed earlier. To cover the rest of the deficits, the federal government has to borrow money. From whom? From rich people, both here in the US and overseas. Thank goodness again for those rich people. They are always there when you need them.

Aha, you say, but how does it pay them back? Well, by and large, it doesn't. Our federal debt over the years has grown more and more. It pays back some people, but always finds even more other people to borrow from. The debt keeps growing, but so does our economy, thank goodness. As a result the annual debt payments remain a relatively small percent of the overall US economy. It is manageable, at least for the time being.

Of course, borrowing has its limits, too. If pushed too far, the government begins to compete with private business for loans. That results in higher interest rates. Of course, it could create more money, but as discussed earlier that would lead to more inflation. The result either way is that we would have higher interest rates and severe inflation, and all the bad things that go with it. The worst thing that happens is that people stop saving money. They spend the money quickly before it loses value. That means that there is no money for investing in the productivity boosters in our economy. That means our productivity stops growing. Very bad indeed, as we well know from previous chapters.

So, you might ask, is it ever good to run a deficit? Yes, it's okay in two circumstances: (1) if it doesn't cause excessive inflation, and (2) if it is needed to stimulate the economy. Wait a minute, you might say, I don't quite understand. Quite simple really. If the economy is in a recession, the government would normally reduce taxes or increase spending to stimulate growth. Remember that? Okay. Well, if that action causes the deficit to increase, is it good or bad? It is both, but mainly good. Why? Because the primary role of the government at such times is to make the economy grow, and get people off unemployment. That's it, plain and simple.

The other side of the coin, however, is that after the economy is growing nicely again, it is highly desirable to have some years of surplus. We had a few such years in the late 1990's and early 2000's, so it is possible. We actually knocked down the federal debt a bit. In the future, this balanced approach of alternating deficits and surpluses will probably be necessary to avoid an excessive federal debt, and all the bad things that result.

That's it. That's all I have to say about monetary and fiscal policy. Now you know what it means and you know roughly how it works. Right?

Well, let's find out. It's time for a short quiz. It is early 2003, and the economy is sputtering. Growth is nearly zero, and unemployment is going up. Inflation is very low. The Fed has already used its monetary policy to reduce interest rates to the lowest level in 40 some years. The government is running a slight deficit. What would you do if you were in charge of the government? Decrease taxes? Increase federal spending? Maybe some of both? Very good. Stimulate the economy. Of course! And since inflation is very low, you have to concern yourself mainly with increasing growth. That was easy. Right? In fact, that is exactly what the Bush administration did in 2003. Decrease taxes and increase spending. You may not agree with how they did it, giving most of the tax cuts to the rich, but directionally they did the right thing.

Wait a minute, you're not finished. Don't forget, once the economy gets rolling, you have to generate some surpluses in order to control the federal debt. Increase some taxes or cut spending, or both, if necessary. Otherwise, your next problem could be much worse--slow growth and high inflation at the same time. It's called "stagflation". We've had some years like that, particularly during the 1970's, and we don't want to see them again. Okay, now this chapter is really finished.

Chapter 9. Open Trade and Immigration

I could have named this chapter "Trade and Immigration Policy", but "Open Trade and Immigration" suits the actual situation better, so that is the title. Our open trade and immigration policy has benefited our economy so much over the years. How, you might ask? By reducing the cost of goods and services for our citizens. However, it has been hard on some of our least capable citizens. We will look at the pluses and minuses.

You will recall that competition has been mentioned over and over as being good for consumers and the economy. It has brought consumers a wide diversity of high-quality products and services to choose from, at reasonable prices. It has made our economy healthier by promoting investment in productivity-boosting facilities. Open trade introduces yet another source of competition to our domestic market, namely imports from other countries. Because of open trade, we can also export products and services to other countries and compete in those markets, as well. Many companies in our economy rely heavily on import and export trade. Most companies in our country are involved to some degree in import/export trade.

Open trade enables another type of import/export business--the free flow of money for investment. People in many other countries like to put their money into investments in our country. They do that because the US has an enormous, healthy economy. On the other hand, US citizens and corporations have invested billions of dollars in other countries, in the pursuit of higher profits.

Open trade has clear benefits--lower prices for goods and services--but as indicated earlier, it has some negatives as well. We have to look at both, to be fair.

Perhaps the best example in terms of overall success is the automobile industry. Through most of the 1960's, almost every car on the road was American-made. These cars were not that reliable, the styling seemed to get worse every year, and they were gas-hogs. During the 1970's, we had two oil crises, in which the price of gasoline went up tremendously. Our auto companies reacted slowly, and the Japanese producers jumped into the market feet first. They offered cars with much better gas mileage, and people began to buy them. With the profits from their increased sales, the Japanese improved their designs to provide better reliability on the road. That led to more sales. Then they put their money into better styling and larger cars. You now see the result. There are loads of Japanese cars on our roads, many of which are now produced by Japanese-owned plants located in the US. However, the "Big Three" US producers (GM, Ford, and Chrysler, the last now merged with Daimler-Benz) are still in business, producing cars that compete with the Japanese. Overall, the benefits have gone to the American consumers, who have much better cars to drive, and at reasonable prices. According to a 2003 article in US News and World Report, since 1990, the average cost of the average car has gone down from 29 to 20 workweeks for the average worker. Now that is the main reason to support competition and free trade—better products at lower prices. What a deal.

We have seen similar results in many other industries, such as semiconductors, computers, software, fuels, steel, chemicals, clothing, and even some luxury goods.

The negative side of open trade is that it often leads to loss of jobs. You probably have noticed that almost all clothing, toys, and many other manufactured goods sold here are produced in other countries. The main reason is that these goods are not especially difficult to manufacture with today's equipment. Therefore, they can be produced in developing countries by people with minimal education, who are paid much less than Americans. This has created big problems for a certain class of Americans--the unskilled worker.

Forty years ago, when most things consumed in the US were made here, this class of worker got along just fine. He was typically a member of a union associated with the CIO labor movement. Because of his union membership, he got a decent wage and benefits. He was able to buy a small, but comfortable house, and a car. His employer survived well enough, because he was competing with companies of the same type, with the same type of employees. As the free trade movement picked up steam, however, many workers of this type lost their jobs, because their factories were shut down. They could not compete with the new cheaper imports.

So we apparently had a win-lose situation, at least initially. The American consumer won by getting access to lower-cost merchandise, but the unskilled worker lost. But there was a way out for him. If he got more job training, he could upgrade his skills, and get another job. Many did just that. They realized that they had been actually under-employed--they had been doing jobs that were below their potential. However, many didn't do so well. In some cases, they lived in remote areas without other job opportunities, and refused to relocate for family or other reasons. In other cases, they were uninspired, non-ambitious, or mentally incapable, and drifted into minimum wage jobs. Overall, there were some winners among the unskilled workers, but some permanent losers as well.

There are other areas of concern. We have become increasingly dependent on imported oil. About 60% of our oil supplies come from foreign countries. Most of the oil reserves in the world are concentrated in the Middle East, which is historically a unstable area. Do you think we would have any interest whatsoever in Iraq if it were located in the middle of Africa, rather than right in the middle of the Middle East oil fields? Don't let anyone tell you otherwise, our interest in Iraq is all about oil. Oil is what has financed Saddam's weapons of mass destruction, and we are main contributors, simply because of our thirst for oil. Because of our dependency, we must be intimately involved in that part of the world. I should mention that our involvement there has been fair-minded. We don't have any colonies there, and we pay an open-market price for the oil that is produced there. We just don't want some wacko trying to take over the region.

A further argument against open trade is our loss of capacity in so-called strategic industries. As a result of cheap imports, we have lost our self-sufficiency in such industries as steel, chemicals, and fuel production. The argument goes that, if we have a major world war, we do not have enough capacity in these industries to supply both our domestic needs and our war machine. That indeed appears to be a weakness. But what is the likelihood of a third world war? Highly unlikely, as such a war would probably result in widespread nuclear destruction. No one wants to go down that road.

A lot of Americans link our open trade policy with our open immigration policy. In effect, we are importing not only low-cost goods, but also low-cost labor. They argue that we have been too lax on immigration, especially illegal immigrants. We have indeed been lax. All of the suicidal murderers on 9/11/2002 were temporary visitors—our guests. Some of them had suspect connections to terrorists, and we knew it, but didn't keep an eye on them. On the other hand, if you look around the major US metropolitan areas, you will find that a large percentage of the workers doing construction, lawn work, and other manual labor are mainly immigrants from south of the border. Same thing applies to agricultural regions. Some of those immigrants are undoubtedly illegal, but most of them are legal. In either case, however, they are doing work, building things that might not otherwise be done, improving the standard of living for all of us.

There are positives and negatives. Let's look at some more positives. Because of our large imports of goods, poor people in places like Bangladesh, Indonesia, China, Guatemala, and India now have jobs. One could argue that is better than their having no jobs, and relying on foreign aid, or else starving. Because of free trade, we have closer relationships with people and countries all over the world. Although some people do hate us, such as certain militant Muslims, most foreigners consider us friendly and admire us. Even in countries such as Iran, where the official government line is that we are agents of the devil, many of the young people admire America.

In order to get some overall perspective, we should look at two extremes. On the one hand, there is complete free trade, which is what we are close to having. At the other extreme, there is "Fortress America". We know a lot already about Option 1, free trade, because we have talked about it, and we in fact live it. So let's look at Option 2, Fortress America.

Fortress America is a concept in which we close ourselves off from the rest of the world. All goods and services that we consume are produced here in the good old USA. There is minimal or no travel to other countries and few foreigners are to be found in the US. They are easy to track, because there are so few of them. This situation might sound good to some people, but there would be a lot of problems.

-Because of our limited oil supplies, gasoline would be very expensive, and there would be fewer cars on the road--all GM, Fords, and Chrysler products. Tiny cars. You can forget your beloved Honda Civics, BMW's, Saabs, Camry's, and most of all, your beloved SUV's.

-Clothing and most other manufactured goods would be at least twice as expensive. So would most services.

-Do you like fresh fruits and vegetables in the middle of winter? They would also be twice as expensive, if available at all.

-Eating out would be horrid. There would be no good ethnic restaurants. Just fast food and the insipid stuff that is served up at places like TGI Fridays and Cracker Barrel. Yuck.

-While we'd sitting here with our borders closed, we would have no influence on world events. We were kind of insulated like that before World Wars I and II. Look what happened. It can happen again. If we're not involved, some wacko is going to take over a country, and start trouble. Unlike those earlier days, we now have to worry about weapons of mass destruction, particularly nuclear weapons.

Look, the genie is out of the bottle. Fortress America stinks. It is totally impractical and dangerous in today's world. Better that we stick with open trade and relatively open immigration. We could clean things up a bit, however: Here are some suggestions:

-Provide better training programs and relocation support for workers who lose their jobs due to plant closings or cheap immigrant labor. Unemployment benefits could also be extended to give them time to train up and/or move out. Overall, we all benefit, because most of these Americans will end up with better jobs and will pay their share of taxes.

-Keep better track of all immigrants. Get their fingerprints when they enter the country, and have them register at the local police station, wherever they live. I was required to do just that when I was living in Germany. It was no big deal.

- With regard to illegal immigrants, I would suggest the following solution:

(1) For those illegal workers who are already residents and have jobs and families with them, grant them a new "Class A" type guest worker visa. This visa could be renewable every three years, if the worker remains employed and out of trouble with the law.

(2) For single illegal workers who are already residents and have jobs, grant them a new "Class B" guest worker visa, which is also good for three years and renewable, but prohibits them from bringing any families into the US. A Class B visa can be upgraded to a Class A visa if the worker has established a good work record in our country, and has no legal problems.

(3) To minimize the number of future illegal workers from entering our country undocumented, we should issue Class B guest worker visa applications at our embassies and consulates outside the US. These new visas should be granted only to people who have job sponsors in the US, or to those who win an annual lottery. The number of lottery winners each year should be based on the general need for such workers. Any lottery winner should have enough money upon entering the country to tide him over until he finds a suitable job.

Once this system is in effect, any illegal immigrant found without proper documentation inside our borders should be put onto a plane. We should be nice about it, however, and give him $200 and an application for a Class B guest worker visa as he gets on the plane. He is being punished enough by being forcibly deported. Since he had the ingenuity to get into the country illegally, he probably has the stuff to be a productive member of the work force. Sometimes a slap on the wrist is more appropriate than a club on the head.

Before we leave this chapter, it is worthwhile to address another current situation that has many Americans concerned—the issue of job "outsourcing" to other countries. In the past, most of the jobs lost to open trade were in the manufacturing sector. Now some white collar service jobs are also at risk, such as call answering services, computer programming, and basic engineering. This new trend has been made possible by recent advances in telecommunications and internet, which enable people in places like India to take jobs that were previously based only in the US. That's the negative side. The positive side is that these new low-cost services are enabling US-based companies to reduce their costs, which should lead to lower prices for goods and services. Also, new small US-based companies--and jobs-- are being created that use these services extensively. Overall, the US workers who benefit are those who are able to plan and implement the use of such services. The workers that have lost their jobs have to upgrade or broaden their skills. For example, a programmer or engineer should consider training to become a project manager or a sales representative in his area of expertise.

That's it for open trade and immigration. We need both, and we have proven that we can handle them well--most of the time. Additional measures should be taken so that we handle them better.

Chapter 10. Energy Sources and Energy Policy

In previous chapters, we described our economy as a kind of living organism, with money as the bloodstream, companies as the vital organs, and government as the central nervous system and conscience. We will now complete the anatomy of this awesome creature by describing what energizes it, what makes it move. Just as food is used by our digestive system to power and heat our bodies and minds, various energy forms are used to power and heat our automobiles, homes, factories, schools, cell phones, and other things throughout the economy.

I have indicated earlier that the economy would stop cold if we removed money, the bloodstream. Well, the same applies if we removed, or disrupted our critical energy sources. During the 1970's, we had two major disruptions of oil supplies, first in response to the 1973 Arab-Israeli conflict and then in the late 1970's during the Iranian revolution. The overall impact on our economy was very bad, the results being major recessions and very high inflation. As you will see, we are still very vulnerable to such disruptions. We have to do something about it. More about that later. First, let's learn the ABC's of energy.

ABC'S OF ENERGY

The main sources of energy in the world are oil, coal, natural gas, nuclear power, and various "renewables", roughly in that order. "Renewables" are sources such as hydropower, solar and wind power that continually provide energy gratis from nature-- once equipment is erected to extract that power.

OIL is the premier energy source in the world for a number of reasons. First of all, it is a liquid, and thus easily transportable. If you don't believe it, think how easy it is to gas up at a service station and drive off. Oil is also easy to burn and convert into motive energy. If you don't believe it, start your car and drive away! How difficult was that? Finally, oil is a very concentrated source of energy. If you don't believe it, see how far you can drive on a single tank of gas--hundreds of miles. You, yourself, would need one or two meals before the car would need refilling.

NATURAL GAS is more difficult to handle. If you don't believe it, try to pour some into your gas tank. If you could see it, the gas would go up, rather than down, because it is lighter than air. It is possible to use natural gas as an automobile, bus or truck fuel, but it must be compressed to a high pressure, and your vehicle must have a special high pressure tank. Otherwise, your vehicle would run out of fuel in a very short time. Therefore, use of natural gas as a transportation fuel is limited primarily to urban areas, where the vehicles in question can always be close to special compression/refill stations.

The most common users of natural gas are so-called stationary energy consumers, such as homes, buildings, and power plants. For heating and power generation, natural gas is great stuff. It is very clean-burning, and gas makes a wonderful power plant fuel. More about that later.

COAL is the junk food of energy supplies, and is used primarily for power generation. Why do I say that? Because coal is a solid material, and contains a lot of impurities such as sulfur, mercury, and other nasty chemicals. Burning coal can contaminate the air with sulfur dioxide, which is bad for your eyes and respiratory system. It can also kill trees and fish. Disposal of coal ash (the solid stuff left after you burn coal) is another problem, as it also contains a lot of nasty materials. Nevertheless, coal is the favored fuel for power generation because it is so plentiful and cheap compared to other fuels. During the last several decades in the US, low-sulfur coal from the western states has been replacing high-sulfur eastern (Appalachian) coal in our power plants, which is a good thing for the environment. Also, some plants burning higher sulfur coal have installed flue gas scrubbers that remove the sulfur dioxide and other noxious chemicals from the flue gas. However, that solution creates another problem, because the scrubbing process produces a large amount of solid sludge that must be disposed, i.e., dumped somewhere. Outside the US, coal is widely used as a heating fuel, as well as a power plant fuel, and much of that coal has high sulfur contents. Thus, in developing countries, such as China, India, and even Turkey, coal pollution is a major problem, which is getting worse as those economies grow.

Coal has two other major environmental impacts. Mining coal is a messy business, particularly if it is strip mined. Strip mining is used whenever coal deposits are close to the surface. This process removes the top layer of earth and rock and then digs out the exposed coal. Although strip mining operators are required to restore the disturbed land in most locations, the environment clearly suffers from mining process. There is a major impact on the plants and animals in the area, and streams are often polluted with chemicals from mine runoff.

The second environmental impact is more subtle. Coal is essentially all carbon, unlike oil and gas, which contain both carbon and hydrogen. As a result a calorie of heat from coal burning generates much more carbon dioxide than that from oil or gas. So what's bad about that? Carbon dioxide is a so-called greenhouse gas, which contributes to global warming. Many scientists believe that the earth is undergoing global warming of such a degree from greenhouse gases that the polar ice caps are melting. They are predicting widespread flooding of low-lying coastal regions and islands throughout the world, as well as the widespread enlargement of desert regions. As a result, they are promoting reduced burning of coal world-wide as one major remedy.

Well, how about NUCLEAR POWER? Nuclear power plants generate no greenhouse gases. If you look at one from a distance, you see only a large plume of steam from a cooling tower. Steam is nothing but pure water. No poisonous gases are emitted, and no poisonous chemicals are injected into the local water supply. So what's the problem? Nuclear plants use purified uranium as a power source, and the source of the heat is the controlled decomposition of the radioactive isotope Uranium-235 to other elements, such as plutonium. Yuck. It is, in effect, a slow-acting nuclear reaction, which can become very dangerous if the reaction gets out of hand. Therefore, the design of such plants includes many safeguards to insure that the nuclear reaction does not get out of control, and become an unintentional nuclear bomb.

If this sounds scary, it is. One reactor at Chernobyl in Ukraine actually went out of control in the 1980's. It didn't blow up with a large mushroom cloud, but it did explode and contaminate a large area in that country. A lot of people were killed, either directly from radiation damage, or later from various cancers. In the US, we had a brief runaway reaction at Three-Mile Island in Pennsylvania, also during the 1980's, which vented some radioactive gases into the local environment. No one was killed, but it did scare the hell out of a lot of people. More recently, a nuclear plant near Port Clinton, Ohio was shut down on an emergency basis when a large corrosion hole was unexpectedly discovered in the head of the reactor. That plant was shut down for repairs for over two years. It was started up in March of 2004, and will be subject to extraordinary oversight by the Nuclear Regulatory Commission for several years. The reason for the extraordinary oversight is that both the company running the plant, First Energy, and the NRC, itself, were judged "complacent" for not finding the corrosion hole earlier.

Another problem with nuclear plants is disposal of the solid radioactive waste that is left. As mentioned earlier, it contains plutonium, and is extremely hazardous. Also, it takes at least ten thousand years to become harmless to living things. What do we do with this waste? It is stored at various temporary sites throughout the US--until a final resting place is found for it. Well, actually the federal government has found a place called Yucca Mountain in Nevada, where it wants to put all this nasty stuff. The problem is that the local folks and the state have taken the matter to court, because they don't want this dangerous junk in their back yards. Would you like it in yours?

You can now see why we have not built any new nuclear plants in the US for a few decades. Other countries are still building new ones, here and there. The French and Japanese, in particular, are strong advocates of nuclear power. One reason is that they have improved designs, and they have no significant indigenous energy sources. Perhaps nuclear power could be viewed as the energy source of last resort.

BACK TO OIL?

Because coal and uranium are so nasty, you might ask, why not use oil for generating electricity? Why bother with junk fuels like coal and nuclear? Oil is actually a great power plant fuel--easy to transport and burn-- and it is relatively clean. Well, one problem with oil is it quite expensive compared to the other fuels. Also, oil supplies are limited, and unfortunately, the main reserves of oil are in difficult places.

What do I mean by difficult places? The cheapest and most plentiful supplies are in the Middle East--countries like Saudi Arabia and Iraq. That's not so great. The next best places are not so desirable either--Russia and the other former Soviet republics, such as Kazakhstan and Azerbaijan. Wonderful. Wait! Let's not forget the latest hot spots--offshore Africa, places like Angola and Equatorial Guinea. Whew! Surely there must be other new, big sources that are less dodgy. Right you are. Deep water Gulf of Mexico, deep water Atlantic and Pacific coast, deep water North Sea and the Arctic. And by "deep water", I mean drilling from a platform in water that can be more than a mile deep! The oil is there, but the cost is very high to get it. Middle East oil costs a few dollars a barrel to get out of the ground. Deep water oil can cost up to ten times as much to recover. Arctic oil is also expensive to extract. Oil drilling sites are extremely remote, and much in the way of infrastructure (roads, pipelines, etc.) have to be constructed to get the oil out of the ground and transported to markets. Also, environmentalists go nuts when the subject of arctic oil or gas is raised. They are sure that extraction operations will despoil the pristine environment in places like Alaska. The oil industry has demonstrated, however, that they can get the gas and oil out without any major disruption to wildlife and tundra.

BACK TO NATURAL GAS

Okay, enough on oil for now. Let's get back to natural gas for a moment, and its use as a power plant fuel. Why is it good for that purpose? As already indicated, it is quite clean. Oh, heck. Actually, when it comes directly out of the ground, It Is not so clean. It contains heavier hydrocarbons (oil components) and often poisonous gases like hydrogen sulfide. Fortunately, however, it is usually inexpensive to clean up the gas, and the by-products--oil liquids and sulfur--are valuable and easy to sell.

Okay, it is now cleaned up, and it consists mainly of methane, CH_4, which has a molecular structure of one carbon atom and four hydrogen atoms. Good stuff. When you burn it you get one molecule of carbon dioxide and two molecules of water, and a lot of heat. That's it. Much better than coal or nuclear, with their nasty by-products.

So why else is gas a good fuel for power plants? To understand that we have to back-track a minute to coal, which is the main power plant fuel in the world. In a typical coal-fired power plant, the coal is pulverized into dust and blown into a combustion chamber, where it is ignited. In the upper part of the combustion chamber is a set of pipes, with water flowing through them. As that water progresses through the pipes, it is vaporized into very hot, high-pressure steam. That steam then goes through a turbine that generates electricity. The low pressure exhaust steam is then cooled by air or water rushing over the pipes, and pumped back to the boiler, where it is heated again to high-pressure steam. This cyclic process works very well, but it has one major shortcoming--it is very inefficient. Only about one third of the heat from the burning coal is converted into electricity. The rest of it goes into the air or a local body of water. You are probably shocked at this inefficiency, but it is sadly the most economic way to generate power from coal.

Now, with natural gas, it is possible to achieve about 50% efficiency. By itself, it doesn't look so great, but it is a lot better than 33%, right? So, how is it possible to get much more from natural gas than from coal? I'll tell you how. The natural gas is first ignited in a combustion chamber. The hot, high-pressure gases pass through a gas turbine, similar to the operation of a jet aircraft engine. The lower-pressure hot gases then pass into another chamber over a set of pipes with water flowing through them, similar to what happens in a coal-fired plant. As in the coal-fired plant, the water turns to steam, and drives another set of turbines.

You can now see why natural gas power plants are more efficient than coal-fired plants-- because there is a two-stage process for extracting energy, versus only one for coal. You are undoubtedly asking, "Why not use the two-stage process for coal as well?" The answer--coal is a solid and would quickly destroy the first-stage turbines. How? By erosion and deposits of coal ash on the turbine blades. Too bad.

Natural gas has still another advantage--which oil does not. Natural gas is more plentiful, and can be found in many places around the world. The US has a lot of gas, and what it can't supply at any particular time, it imports from Canada. There is also a large amount of gas in Alaska that can't be tapped yet, because a pipeline is needed to transport it across Canada to the lower 48. Whenever it is built, it would run parallel to the existing oil pipeline from Alaska.

HOW ABOUT RENEWABLES?

How about those renewable sources of energy, such as hydropower, wind, and solar? Many environmentalists love this stuff, but there are problems. Hydropower is a significant source of energy wherever you find fast-moving streams in mountainous areas. The problem is that you must build a dam to maintain a steady source of water to get through seasonal variations in natural flow. What do I mean by that? There's a much stronger flow in the spring, when the snow melts, than in the late summer when there is little rainfall. Power plants need a steady source of energy to run efficiently--in this case, water flow. Hence the need for dams. The problem with dams is that fish can't swim upstream past them to spawn. Also, large areas are flooded by the construction of the dam, and many animals and plants lose their homes. Many times, those animals are people, and you must pay them off. Overall, hydropower has limited economic application due to geography, and it causes environmental problems, as described above.

Wind power is just beginning to take off. (Ha, ha). No joke, really. In the past, some wind towers have been constructed to generate electricity, with federal government subsidies. You can see them in some areas of California, and along the Pennsylvania turnpike near Somerset. The latest generation of wind towers is reportedly competitive with coal and gas in certain areas of the country. Therefore, we may see many more of them in the future, in windy places. What are the drawbacks of wind power? First of all, the supply of wind is not constant, as we all know, so a wind tower cannot be a sole source of electricity. You need a backup supply. Secondly, wind towers are unsightly, noisy, and have been known to kill careless birds. Whack! Similar to hydropower, wind power has limited economic application due to geography, and it has environmental drawbacks as well.

Solar power works, when the sun is shining. During night time or cloudy days, the output drops dramatically. Therefore, like wind power, you need backup. Backup can either be an alternate source of power, or a battery that is charged when the sun is shining. Solar power cannot yet compete with coal or gas economically, except in very remote areas, where there are no power lines.

Solar heating works well enough, even when it's cloudy. You can find homes and businesses scattered throughout the country that are heated by solar radiation.

Again, like hydro and wind power, solar energy has limited economic application, largely determined by geographical location.

Okay, at this point, you might be thinking, "What does he mean exactly when he says 'limited economic application'?" This is the type of hocus pocus argument raised by big business honchos when they argue with environmentalists. Well, it works like this. Whenever you want to build a facility for generating power from renewables such as wind, water, or sunlight, you have to invest in rather expensive equipment to do so, such as dams, wind towers or solar arrays made of silicon. How do you pay for such equipment? You could borrow money from a bank, as many businesses do. But you will surely remember, you have to pay off that loan, just as you have to pay off your car loan. In order to do so, your new renewables power plant must pay a profit high enough to cover your annual bank loan payments. Remember? Revenues minus costs for the plant must be enough to make loan payments (principle plus interest). Well, in many cases--most cases actually--the estimated profit is not enough to pay off the bank loans. Therefore, the facility is not built. Got that? Good. But do not give up on renewables. As technology advances, renewables will find more attractive economic applications. Again, that is one of the wonders of our open free market economy.

Okay, that's it for the ABC's of energy. I hope you were able to plow through it, and understand it. Now we can get into the important issues of energy supply and demand.

KEY ENERGY SUPPLY AND DEMAND ISSUES

The US has been well endowed with energy sources. Throughout the years, we have produced most of what we consumed. We have enough coal to last hundreds of years at current usage rates. However, when it comes to oil and gas, things have been getting worse, rather than better. In recent decades our demands are outpacing our domestic supplies.

According to the Energy Information Administration (a branch of the federal government, which will be the main source of data in this section), the US consumes about 20 MMBD (million barrels per day) of oil. Crude oil is fed to oil refineries throughout the country, which separate and refine it into various products. By product, the main demands are for gasoline (45%), diesel/heating oil (19 %), and jet fuel (8%). The remaining 28% of demand is for a variety of other oils, such as industrial/power plant fuel, lubricants, solvents, LPG etc. About 60% of US total oil demand is imported. The main suppliers are Canada, Saudi Arabia, Mexico, and Venezuela, each of which provides 1.5-2.0 MMBD. Roughly 40% of our oil imports come from OPEC, the international oil cartel of producing countries, which is dominated by Middle East producers. Are you getting uncomfortable? Good. You should be.

With regard to natural gas, we are in much better shape. Our total consumption is 23.2 TCF (trillion cubic feet), and we import 15% of that, primarily from Canada (90+ %) via pipeline.

Overall, oil provides 39 % of our total energy needs, natural gas and coal each about 23-24%, and nuclear and renewables each about 7-8%. Our main problem is oil supply and demand, and that is the main area of focus during the rest of this chapter.

KEY POLITICAL ISSUES

We, the American people, have a very strong economy. It is by far the most flexible and innovative economy in the world. Because of this strong economy, we are able to field the strongest military in the world. What could go wrong? As indicated earlier we have one big economic problem, a true Achilles heel that seems to be getting worse, year by year. That problem is oil. Again, as indicated earlier, we depend on imports for 60% of our oil supplies. Most of the oil reserves in the world are concentrated in the Middle East and other potentially unstable areas. Our experience in the Middle East has shown that oil revenues can be used in very bad ways. Oil money was the means for Colonel Ghaddafi in Libya to pursue and support terrorist acts, including the downing of two large commercial airliners in the 1980's. Oil money was the means for Saddam Hussein to kill over a million people in the Middle East, including hundreds of thousands of his own people in Iraq. Oil money flowing into Saudi Arabia was the means for Al Queda to get started and propagate throughout the Muslim world. Oil money has been a means for Hamas and other terrorist organizations to plan and execute suicide bombings in Israel. Oil money supports the regime of a leftist crackpot in Venezuela, who is making life miserable for only his own people, as far as we know.

At this point, let me ask you an important question. How much does a barrel of imported oil cost us? Offhand, you probably don't know, and would look it up on CNBC or the internet. If you did your homework right, you would come up with the answer, "about $30 per barrel". Indeed, that is the going rate on the international oil market. However, it is the wrong answer. Dead wrong. Why?? Iit does not cover the cost of fighting the international mischief and terrorism that is funded by oil money. When you top up your compact car or your SUV with gas, the cost is a lot more than the $1.50 per gallon indicated on the pump. You are supporting vicious dictators, terrorists, or crackpots somewhere with every gallon that flows

69

into your tank. You are supporting nuclear weapons programs in countries such as Iraq, Libya, and Iran. As a result, we as a country have to spend enormous amounts of money in many different places throughout the world to hold them in check. Homeland security, wars in Afghanistan and Iraq, intelligence and undercover operations in dozens of other countries, billions of dollars in economic and military aid to Israel, Pakistan, the Philippines and many other allies in the war on terror. And yes, the occasional major disaster like 9/11/2001. Do you think we are really safe from another 9/11? If you do, then you do not agree with most experts on the subject. You are living in a dream world.

ALTERNATE SOLUTIONS AND POLICIES

Are you angry? Are you upset? Of course you are. We have to do something, and you have to help. Let's look at some ideas for solving this problem. Since this is a book on economics, I will try to stick mainly to that type of solution. I'll try to leave warfare, diplomacy and intelligence operations largely to others who are more capable. However, I must insist that there is an element of economics even in those areas, and I will touch upon them when necessary, as you will see below.

Okay, our problem is oil. What can we do to alleviate the problem? Let's do a stepwise analysis.

Most of the oil reserves are in the "difficult places" that we mentioned earlier. Why don't we use our war machine to take over some of the largest reserves? For example, we could attack a remote area of Saudi Arabia, cordoned it off, and sell the oil to all buyers at a reasonable price. Why waste hundreds of soldiers' lives in a place like Iraq and get nothing from it, when we could incur much lower casualties in Saudi Arabia, and get a lot of oil supplies under our control? Well, Saudi Arabia is the home of Islam's most holy shrines. Therefore, we would most likely get a wild reaction from the Moslem world, and create armies of Jihadists who would be only too happy to go to their deaths killing Americans. Everyone else in the world would hate us, as well. Our economy would be constantly supporting wars throughout the world. It's a bad idea, really. Let's dump it.

A less aggressive idea is to punish the bad guys who use oil money in bad ways. For example, if Saddam Hussein is a constant threat to the world, let's attack Iraq, and try to install a new and better government. As you know, we have tried to do exactly that. Saddam is sitting in jail, as planned, but we are having a devil of a time installing that new government.

Hundreds of US soldiers have been killed, and thousands seriously injured, and the end is still nowhere in sight. That is a large cost. However, what would the cost have been if Saddam had stayed in power? Perhaps sanctions would have been eventually lifted, and he would again be up to his old tricks. How many Iraqi lives have we saved by putting the old bum in jail, and killing his two monstrous kids? Are Iraqi lives less valuable than American lives? Overall, the real question is how many people would have been killed if he had stayed in power, versus how many people will be killed as a result our war effort? Don't forget that he is already responsible for over a million deaths. I think, deep down, you know the right answer. Go for the option that produces the fewest deaths. That is the economic way to look at warfare. You might argue that only American lives are worth anything. If that is the case, we have already lost thousands all over the world from terrorist acts. Many thousands more will likely follow if we don't pursue and neutralize all the really bad guys—those who actually do the killing, and those who support them, directly or indirectly.

How about the peripheral effects of the Iraqi war? There have been some promising outcomes related to the war effort. Libya's Ghaddafi has given up his weapons of mass destruction, and provided a wealth of information on heretofore secret nuclear proliferation activities throughout the world. Iran has let in international inspectors to monitor their nuclear activities. Even North Korea seems to be more ready to negotiate getting rid of their nuclear weapons.

Overall, the jury is still out on "punishing the bad guys", but it seems to be working. Only time will tell. The main thing to consider is what decision leads to the least number of dead and injured people. I know many of you cannot stand to think about such things, but you have to do it. Successfully demonstrating against the Iraqi war would not have prevented deaths. It would have simply resulted in a different pattern and number of deaths.

Okay, enough about warfare and deaths. There must be other, more peaceful actions we can take to alleviate our oil problem. How can we decrease our imports of foreign oil, while keeping the bad guys in check? What if we did something to dramatically reduce the demand for oil in the world? What would happen? Experience has shown that the international oil market prices are actually quite sensitive to demand variations. Several times in the past, oil prices have dropped a lot due to world-wide recessions and oil conservation efforts following oil supply disruptions. Most OPEC countries, such as Nigeria, Indonesia, and Venezuela are relatively poor, with large populations. Saudi Arabia and Kuwait are the exceptions, not the rule, in OPEC. When demand has dropped in the past, these poorer countries have cheated, and produced more than their agreed OPEC quotas. This cheating has led to gluts of oil supply and lower oil prices.

We have here the roots of a possible solution. Lower demand would reduce our oil imports, oil prices would drop, and the bad guys would have much less money to play with. But it won't be easy. Otherwise we would have already done it. I will table some recommendations below. See how you like them. I'm sure President Bush and a number of other Republicans (e.g., Dick Cheney) will not like some of them.

Basically, we can reduce imports of oil by increasing our own production, or reducing our demand, or both. Bush and company seem to prefer the former, but I think the latter has much more potential.

-Two Japanese car companies, Toyota and Honda, have shown that so-called hybrid engine technology works. Hybrid cars are powered by both an electric motor and a gasoline engine. The fuel supply is 100% gasoline, but motive power is provided by both the motor and the engine. How is that possible? The gas mileage of these vehicles is much higher than conventional gas-only vehicles. Why? Because the electic motor is charged when the car needs braking power, whether going down a hill or stopping at a light. Instead of motive energy being converted to heat, as in a conventional car's brakes, the energy is used to charge a battery that later drives the electric motor. That's one advantage behind the hybrid technology. Another relates to city driving. In a normal car, you waste a lot of fuel idling at stop lights, and traveling in low gear. In a hybrid, your gasoline engine is largely shut down in town, and you run on the electric motor. Cool, huh? Well, it's simple on the surface, but it is technically challenging to implement, and possible only because of recent advances in electronic microprocessors and other technologies. Again, competition among corporations has created another wonderful, new type of product.

So what can hybrids do for us? Well, the existing compact hybrid sedans operate on 50-55 miles per gallon versus 30-35 for conventional vehicles of the same type. Other, larger vehicles are on the way, including SUV's, from American companies, as well as the Japanese. The hybrid SUV's would operate on 25-30 miles per gallon versus the conventional 15-20 miles per gallon. Overall, if we could instantly convert all cars to hybrid technology, they would consume 1/3 less gasoline. With US gasoline demand currently at about 9MMBD, hybrids could knock demand down by 3MMBD. This is a large number compared to our current oil production (8 MMBD) and our imports (over ll MMBD). It is certainly large compared to any new oil reserve we are likely to find in the US.

Anyhow, that's what's possible in the US. How about the rest of the world? There's a lot of potential there, as well, because the rest of the world uses three times more oil than the US. Hybrids are certainly the way to go--the cars of the future--and today--here and everywhere.

Any other ideas? Let's put some down and discuss them briefly.

-How about hybrids for diesel trucks and buses? Well, you can't turn diesels off and on like a gasoline engine, so you lose some of the hybrid technology advantage. But it's worth a look.

-For short runs in urban areas, both trucks and buses can run on compressed natural gas (CNG) with the right infrastructure. In Washington, DC, all of the new buses are burning CNG. This is definitely worth pursuing on a national basis to reduce the consumption of diesel oil.

-Many members of Congress (from farm states, of course) are pushing the use of ethanol in gasoline, and many gas stations in the country are using it. Unfortunately, ethanol is expensive to produce from corn (the usual source), and the last I heard, requires more energy to produce than it produces in your car. Also, the US taxpayer (you!) pays a subsidy of about 50 cents per gallon for ethanol blended into gasoline. This is clearly a last-resort type of solution, but it works to reduce oil imports somewhat.

-More areas could be opened to oil exploration and production, in particular, "sensitive" areas. These include offshore California and Florida, and Alaskan wildlife preserves. While environmentalists are very much against exploitation of these possible oil reserves, there must be a way to do it without spoiling them. After all, Alaska was not greatly disrupted by exploitation of the North Slope reserves. That was successfully done several decades ago, and technology has improved substantially since then to minimize potential environmental damage.

-Generally speaking, more energy conservation is possible throughout the economy. For example, I have a gas furnace in my home that has an efficiency of over 90%, some 20% improvement on the standard furnace.

If enough oil-burning homes were converted to this type of furnace, there would be a significant reduction in oil demand. I'm sure there are many similar commercial and industrial opportunities for reducing oil consumption as well.

Okay, overall, there are a lot of ways to decrease our imports of oil. Clearly the most promising is the use of hybrid technology in vehicles. But there are a number of other ways, including opening up sensitive areas to oil exploration and production. How do we get things moving quickly? Let's use the federal government as a tool for expediting matters:

-Promote hybrid technology and oil conservation in vehicles by (1) raising the fuel efficiency (CAFÉ) standards for cars, SUV's and light trucks, (2) progressively raising the federal gasoline tax, and (3) using the increased tax revenue to subsidize the purchase of new hybrids and the junking old, inefficient vehicles.

-Establish federal tax subsidies for specific energy conservation investments in commerce and industry, and conversion of truck and bus fleets from diesel fuel to CNG.

-Provide federal funding for basic research and subsidies on promising technologies to both increase US energy supplies and expand the usage of energy conservation. On the supply side, one technology being pushed by the Bush administration (and many others) is country-wide use of hydrogen. One way to produce it would be to react coal, water, and air, a proven, but very expensive process. While promising in some respects, the economics of this option are questionable, and a hydrogen economy is decades in the future, if ever. Another promising technology would be to improve the fermentation process so that lower-grade organic materials, such as leaves (i.e., cellulose), could be converted to ethanol. Leaves are a much cheaper raw material than corn.

In summary, the proposed methods of dealing with our current oil crisis are (1) go after the bad guys, wherever they are, while promoting transitions to peaceful regimes in those countries, (2) promote the use of energy-saving technology, in particular hybrid vehicles, (3) facilitate exploration and production of oil in the US in an environmentally responsible manner, and (4) promote promising new technologies and sources of energy, such as advanced fermentation methods to produce lower-cost ethanol.

Chapter 11. Children

This is the last chapter of this book. Thank goodness, huh? But, children? What in the world do children have to do with economics? Well, if you think about it, plenty. Children are the future adults. They are the future workers. They will be paying your social security and Medicare entitlements when you are old and decrepit, and can no longer work. They will be the future managers, governors, criminals, teachers, soldiers, and Presidents of the United States. Yes, children are very important little economic creatures. Let's look at some of the ways that we can make sure that our children become hard-working, productive adults.

EDUCATION

We have one of the best education systems in the world. That is indirectly obvious from the fact that we are by far the leading economic country in the world. I do see some trouble spots, however, that could get worse, so we should recognize them and address them.

One of these is ESL, English as a Second Language education. This is extremely important because it mainly involves the children of our largest immigrant group, the Spanish-speaking folks from Mexico, Central America, and South America. In the good old days, any foreign kid had to learn English fast, because that's what was spoken in the schools. With the advent of ESL, we now have bilingual teachers, who speak Spanish as well as English. While well-intentioned, the result is that many of the kids in ESL classes don't learn much English at all. Also, many of the ESL teachers are not very good teachers. So the other result is that many of these kids leave the school system under-educated.

I know a kid who was making A's in a certain school. He was in the ESL program. He did well in his arithmetic class. His teacher wanted to hold him back in that class, and not go into algebra for a year. Why? So that he could be a good example for the kids in the arithmetic class and help them. Does that make sense to you? I hope not. As it turned out, he couldn't even do fractions well.

I know this kid well. He is my adopted son. My wife and I adopted him at the time he was in that school. We got him out of that school, and into better ones. That school is in Washington, DC.

I'm sure there are other schools like that, schools that for one reason or another are not working. We need to find them and fix them or shut them down. How? A good start is for all students to undergo regular mandatory standardized testing. That way, we can follow their progress, and the progress of the schools they attend. Some liberals don't like standardized testing. I do. However, I admit it can be overdone. I think it should be done only in the three R's- reading, writing and arithmetic. Once a kid masters these basics, he is ready to take on any of the higher subjects such as history, algebra and geometry, and so on. And he is ready to take on most entry-level jobs! Also he is doing much better than 37 % of the adults in Washington, DC.

I also take the non-liberal position of favoring the use of education vouchers. In many poor inner-city schools, there are children who really want to learn, and their parents want them to learn. Problem is those parents don't have the money to send them elsewhere--to a school with a better learning environment, where they won't be pressured by gangs and drug dealers into bad behavior. If they had vouchers, they would likely end up in a parochial school, a school with a religious affiliation, like Catholic or Methodist. Some liberals go ballistic with the thought of it. Using public money to send a kid to a religious school! Outrageous! However, where does that public money come from in the first place? It comes from taxpayers, like the parents who want the vouchers. Why shouldn't they have more rights in this matter than some detached liberal, who likely went to private school or a good school in a well-to-do neighborhood? Not convinced? Look at it another way. Would you prefer that a kid become a criminal or a Methodist? Still not convinced? Forget it. You're hopeless.

I would like to close this section with some positive comments. It is truly remarkable to me how many kids from low-income families in our country are able to get themselves educated and become highly-skilled workers or professionals--doctors, lawyers, engineers, scientists. We have a wonderful system in which all sorts of help is available for kids to get themselves educated. We have low-cost junior colleges, where kids can get associate degrees, or a two-year jump on a four-year degree. We have all types of financial aid available--Pell grants, low-interest loans, scholarships. Many of these scholarship funds were set up by rich folks. That's right. As I mentioned earlier, I got a full scholarship in chemical engineering at Cornell University, thanks to a generous fellow by the name of McMullen.

If a child is willing to work hard and has a reasonable living situation, he can really do well in this country, regardless of the economic status of his parents. No other country can match the opportunity that is offered in the good, old US of A. Amen.

BAD PARENTS

There is nothing worse for a child's future than bad parents. We all know that they exist. They are a primary cause of criminal behavior in our society. If a child is badly abused or neglected or has poor role models, it is less likely that he will grow up to be a productive citizen. We all know that. Most of us do nothing much about it but wring our hands, and call the cops if one of them threatens us. By then it is probably too late to help them, so you might as well call the cops.

So what kinds of bad parents do we have? We had a lot of "welfare parents" for many decades. The government figured way back that many parents were beyond repair. So we might as well give the family some money to live on so the kids wouldn't starve. They didn't starve, but many of the kids grew up to be criminals and social misfits. These children had no access to good role models, so many of them became welfare recipients as well. No skills, no desire to do better. They couldn't even envisage themselves as productive members of society. This was a case of government-supported bad parenting. And to make the situation worse, the government policy of the time encouraged the fathers of these children to live away from the family.

Well, we kind of woke up during the last several decades. A certain program called "Head Start" was initiated, which focused on helping the children from such families in pre-school programs. Later, welfare policy itself underwent a radical change, led by the governors of such states as Wisconsin, and later taken up by the federal government. Without going into a lot of detail about individual programs, the main policies that seem to work are as follows:

-For parents who are mentally and physically capable, welfare payments became limited to several years. During that time, the recipients are expected to get themselves trained up to get a job. Governments have worked together to provide support for various job training programs, including getting an equivalent high school diploma (GED).

-Various free day-care programs have been initiated for the children of these parents. While the child is in day care, the parent can do job training, take a job, or both.

-The federal government initiated the "earned income credit" program for very low income families. As mentioned in a previous chapter, such families get a tax refund that can be more than they had paid in during the year. The amount of the refund goes down as the family income goes up. But you get nothing unless you do at least some part-time work.

Overall, these programs have been successful in getting welfare parents into the work force. Let me give you an example. I knew personally a young Hispanic woman who had two children, born when she was 16 and 17 years old-- a teen mother. At an early age, her kids went into free day care. According to the rules, she had to provide evidence from time to time that she was working or training. She never worked full-time, but kept taking jobs to keep her kids in free day care. She also worked because she got a wonderful check every year from the federal government.

How are her kids doing? Fine. They are now attending public school. They are good kids, and I think they are going to make it.

I should mention that this young mother had a lot of support from our family--my wife, in particular. My wife helped her navigate through all of the agencies that provide aid, and introduced her to the earned income tax credit. You see, the government can't do it all. Private citizens can participate in the process with some hands-on help. So get out and do it. Be a true liberal.

Now, getting back to the issue of bad parenting, there is another type who might not be poor at all, but has a serious psychological problem. It could be a full-fledged psychosis, or a profound personality defect. This situation is much more common than you think. Whichever ailment it is, the children can be badly affected. They can be severely abused--mentally, as well as physically.

Another type of bad parent can be simply neglectful. With both parents working in many families these days, children in some cases are getting little care or guidance from their parents

What should we do in cases like this? In the case of a mentally disturbed parent, there are two possibilities. If the other parent is normal, which is usually the case, we should provide all of the support that we can for that parent. In the schools, guidance counselors should be trained to work with them and provide special counseling to the children. Furthermore, there is a strong case here for long-term welfare payments to the family, as the normal parent might have to care for the disturbed parent much of the time.

In the courts, judges should be trained to identify abnormal behavior that could be harmful to a child. Many times, child custody disputes are between a normal parent and a disturbed parent. Obviously, the normal parent should get custody, regardless of the sex of that parent. The odds of that happening are greatly improved if the judge is able to spot a mental illness.

What do you do if both parents are mentally disturbed? You find the child a new family as soon as possible. There really is a point where the rights of parents have to be subordinate to the rights of a helpless child. I hate to agree with Newt Gingrich, but he was right when he indicated that an orphanage can be better for a child than really bad parents.

With regard to the "simply neglectful" parent, there are several things that can be done, but my favorite is after-school programs. You can find some out there already. There are the YMCA and church programs. Even some schools have programs. Washington, DC has the Latin American Youth Center, which is a wonderful place for young Hispanics to hang out. Unfortunately, it has recently lost some federal funding. Thank you, President Bush.

That's about it for my commentary on children. They need help to pursue and get a good education. They need help if their parents are not doing a good job of parenting. Finally, they need help if their parents are poor.

But there is one other important point. What can you do to help out? You figure it out. Use your time, money and effort to do whatever you can. If you're not a hands-on type of person, make contributions, or do volunteer work of a different type, such as office support. There are many possibilities. Go do it.

On that note, I will inform you that you have reached the end of this book. I had a good time writing it. I hope you have enjoyed it, and learned something. Most of all, I hope the book will stimulate your thinking about all of the important subjects that we have covered, and that you will be a better citizen for it. Get out there and help revive the Democrat party. Make your contribution to the health and prosperity of our country. And most important, help the people who need it the most, especially kids.

About The Author

After acquiring a bachelor's degree in chemical engineering and an MBA, Ben Arbutiski worked in the oil business for 30 years, performing consulting work throughout the world. He has used this experience to write a book that describes, in everyday language, how a successful economy operates, and what strategies our Democratic leadership should pursue on key economic issues. He is hopeful that the book will be an inspiration to young Democrats, and that it will be helpful in renewing the original optimistic spirit of the Democratic party--to build a strong America, to help the unfortunate live a comfortable life, and to help the able achieve their highest potential.